C000118301

Trust

Trust

Alphonso Lingis

University of Minnesota Press

Minneapolis — London

THEORY OUT OF BOUNDS

Edited by Sandra Buckley, Michael Hardt, and Brian Massumi

Volume 25

"Araouane" was originally published in the *Antioch Review* 60, no. 1 (winter 2000): 87–93.

"Love Junkies" was originally published as "Armed Assault" in *Aesthetic Subjects,* edited by Pamela R. Matthews and David McWhirter (Minneapolis: University of Minnesota Press, 2003).

All photographs in the book were taken by the author, with the exception of the following. The photograph accompanying "Unknowable Intelligence" is reprinted courtesy of Marilyn Bridges. The photograph accompanying "A Man" is reprinted courtesy of Editora Política, Havana, Cuba; it appeared in Fernando Diego García and Óscar Sola, *Che Sueño Rebelde* (Madrid: Celeste Ediciones, 1997). The photograph accompanying "Lalibela" is reprinted courtesy of Carol Beckwith and Angela Fisher; copyright Carol Beckwith and Angela Fisher.

Copyright 2004 by the Regents of the University of Minnesota

All rights reserved. No part of this publication may be reproduced, stored in a retrieval system, or transmitted, in any form or by any means, electronic, mechanical, photocopying, recording, or otherwise, without the prior written permission of the publisher.

Published by the University of Minnesota Press
111 Third Avenue South, Suite 290
Minneapolis, MN 55401-2520
http://www.upress.umn.edu

Library of Congress Cataloging-in-Publication Data

Lingis, Alphonso, 1933–
    Trust / Alphonso Lingis.
        p.   cm. — (Theory out of bounds ; v. 25)
    Includes bibliographical references.
    ISBN 0-8166-4372-5 (alk. paper) — ISBN 0-8166-4373-3 (pbk. : alk. paper)
    1. Lingis, Alphonso, 1933– —Travel. 2. Voyages and travels. I. Title. II. Series.
    G465.L563 2004
    910.4—dc22

                                                            2003028182

Printed in the United States of America on acid-free paper

The University of Minnesota is an equal-opportunity educator and employer.

19 17 16 15 14 13 12 11   10 9 8 7 6 5 4 3 2

Contents

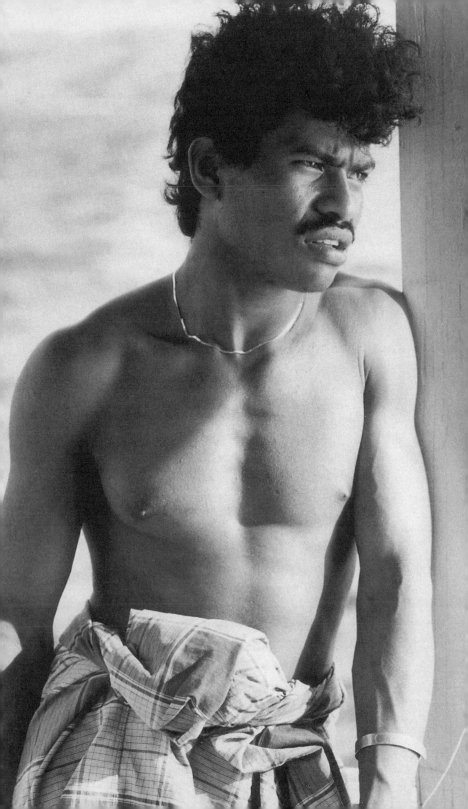

Preface

O N A WALK IN THE RAIN FOREST we come upon an
orchid; it spreads the trembling contours of its petals
before us and unreservedly fills our eyes with the tones and
glow of its colors. However completely the orchid had been
described to us, the moment we see it with our own eyes there
is shock, astonishment, and discovery. We station ourselves on
Antarctic cliffs to watch the penguins scramble up the rookery
and each locate its own baby, we descend into the oceans to
watch the fish that dwell in different niches in the coral reefs
and different depths of the waters. That the great whales sing
like birds has been only recently discovered by biologists, for
their songs do not pass out of the water into the air. Modern
recording technology has transferred these songs to phono-
graph disks so that we can hear them with our ears across the
air of our living rooms. But when we descend into the ocean
with the whales we find ourselves immersed in song; our whole
bodies, themselves mostly composed of water, reverberate
with melodies in the substance of water. All there is to know
about the ancient cities now in ruins, about gods long forgotten whose temples are now protected and even meticulously
restored, we get from the words and images of books and
videotapes. But we go to linger among the stones and there
make contact with what, though long past, is still there and
sacred. We go for the shock, astonishment, and discovery.

In the great rookeries the penguins locate their own babies from among thousands by their distinctive voiceprint. In the forests we learn to identify unseen birds by their songs. But when we go to different places inhabited by members of our own species, what our eyes see of them and of the places they inhabit is blurred by the language that fills those places and that we do not understand—and even if we do. Is it not because what they say is but babble to us that what our eyes see of them, their facial contours, complexions, and garb, look exotic to us? And when someone there is standing before us, speaking directly to us, we have been cautioned that he is not speaking with his own voice but speaking the language of his gender, his family, his class, his education, his culture, his economic and political interests, his unconscious drives, indeed his state of physical health and alertness. The effort to know him gets detoured into efforts, ever more evidently fragmentary and superficial, to know all these layers. Today the professionals who study these things write books exposing how superficial and deluded have been the efforts of the experts: exposing the imperialist, Christian, Victorian, romantic, or orientalist fables written by those people who left their homelands and fell in love in some remote place, married, and never returned; the positivist, Freudian, or Marxist fables of the past generation of cultural anthropologists; the rationalist, structuralist, or postmodern fables of the current generation.

How often am I aware that others are only dealing with some role I occupy in a society, some pantomime I am performing, some set of clothes and haircut I am wearing! They see and address the American, the professor, or the decently dressed restaurant client, while *I* am thinking for myself and acting on my own, behind that image they see!

Yet it does happen that someone exterior to me approaches and makes contact with *me*—the real me, the core me, whatever I can take to be *me*. It happens every day that I feel a force that breaks out of the passing forms and takes hold of me:

"Hey you!" "Hey Al!" Isn't it astounding—really our theories do not account for it—that I feel these words coming straight at me, hitting me, clamping on to *me*? An appeal is being addressed to *me*, a demand put on *me*. The words have penetrated right through the role, the social identity, the visible and interpretable form, to the very core that is *me*. Each time I do answer on my own, I have acknowledged that that is what has happened.

Every day we deal with people who occupy posts in the established social system where behaviors are socially defined and sanctioned. We rely on the bus driver following the scheduled route, we count on the bank teller giving us proper credit for our mortgage payment. Our confidence in the actions of these people is based on our knowledge of how the transportation or commercial system works. But to *trust you* is to go beyond what I know and to hold on to the real individual that is you. In listening to the several surgeons I consult about my condition, I become confident that the one or the other speaks as a representative of the state of the art of surgical methods and techniques. But the trust I extend to the one I choose to do the surgery is a bond with the real individual she is, whose insights and motives I do not see and in whom there is the possibility of ignorance and incompetence, mendacity and malevolence. When we leave our home and community to dwell awhile in some remote place, it happens every day that we trust a stranger, someone with whom we have no kinship bonds, no common loyalty to a community or creed, no contractual obligations. We have no idea what he said, what are his family, clan, and village coordinates, the categories with which he represents for himself society, nature, and the cosmos. We attach to someone whose words or whose movements we do not understand, whose reasons or motives we do not see. Our trust short-circuits across the space where we represent socially defined behaviors and makes contact with the real individual agent there—with *you*.

Once one determines to trust someone, there is not simply a calm that enters into one's soul; there is excitement and exhilaration. Trust is the most joyous kind of bond with another living being. But isn't it true that whenever we enjoy being with someone, there is a factor of risk there, and also a factor of trust, which gives our enjoyment an edge of rapture?

Fear contains a recognition of the dangerous and destructive force of something or someone approaching or possibly lurking ahead. Fear deepens as our imagination multiplies representations of the danger. We seek to dissipate the fear by representing the danger as unreal and by representing our knowledge, implements, and skill to deal with what is ahead as effective and assured. But it happens that the ideas one has fashioned about death, representing it as remote or as unreal, a sleep or a transition, break up, and one is faced with death itself.

What does one see when one faces death? Death will wipe away all there is to see in the landscape about one, in the irreversible extinction of one's individual existence. One sees the indeterminate and interminable abyss, nothingness itself. One feels it ready to gape open under every path that looks unstable, under every tool in one's hand that one senses may malfunction or break up. What feels this imminence of the abyss is the anxiety that throbs in the very core of what one is. Yet as death closes in, courage can arise from some unknown depth of oneself. Courage is a force that can hold one resolute and lucid as death itself approaches.

Courage and trust have this in common: they are not attitudes with regard to images and representations. Courage is a force that can arise and hold steadfast as one's projections, expectations, and hopes dissipate. Courage rises up and takes hold and builds on itself. Trust is a force that can arise and hold on to someone whose motivations are as unknown as those of death. It takes courage to trust someone you do not know. There is an exhilaration in trusting that builds on itself. One really cannot separate in this exhilaration the force of trust and the force of courage.

Laughter and sexual attraction are also forces that break through images and representations. Laughter is released by the outbreak of incoherence in discourse, the breakup of meaning, by awkward, bungling efforts, and by goals that collapse when one has laboriously reached them. The peals of laughter hold on to the moment when the past that gave drive and skill to movements breaks off, when the future that gave sense and purpose to words and actions disconnects. There is just left the present, the naked and meaningless things, the thrashings of bodies—and the excess energies of the one who laughs. The energies ricocheting off the raw things fuel the peals of laughter.

At the same time laughter is contagious, a force that passes through the boundaries of individual identities. The anthropologist, who has worked out in a fitness club for a year in preparation for the rigors of the field, advances with bold steps over the log fallen over the river; halfway across he slips, tries to grab the log as he holds on to his video camera, and lurches into the water and muck below. Still holding high his camera draining muddy water, he looks up and sees laughter spreading in waves across the natives he had come to ingratiate and study. He feels the immediacy and the reality of their presence in the force of the shared laughter. He laughs with them, with their hilarity.

Erotic impulses are excited by all the artifices of adornment and masquerade. Sensuality is aroused by the intense colors of sumptuous garments and by jewelry whose metal and crystal glitter across naked flesh; it is ensnared by the suggestive shiftings of someone's eyes, his or her pirouetting fingers, provocative poses, and gamy words. But the fascination with these seductive appearances and accoutrements unleashes lustful drives that crave to break through the images to take hold of and penetrate the anonymous animal body behind them. The sexual craving that torments us shuts us off to the projects and solicitations of the common and practicable world, but it is also anonymous and spreads by contagion, making us transparent to one another. In Salvador in Brazil during Carnaval a couple are dancing clad in the tuxedo and the white wedding gown in which they were married, in this street during Carnaval thirty years ago. As they dance they embrace and disrobe one another, revealing under the tuxedo the naked body of a woman, under the wedding gown the naked body of a man. Our eyes are held on them and fevered and feel a current of complicity with the crowd about us, men and women, white and black, adolescent and aged.

In the way that laughter and sexual craving break through the images and representations and labeling of things and make contact with the singular reality, they have a kinship with courage and with trust. Indeed, just as there is courage in trust, so there is pleasure, exhilaration in trust: trust laughs at dangers. And sexual attraction is so like trust: it careens toward sexual surrender to another as into an unconditional trust. Conversely, there is something erotic in trust, for trust is not a bare thrust of will holding on to the unintelligible core of another; it holds on to the sensibility and forces of another. There is something erotic in the trust that a skydiver extends to his buddy plummeting after him bringing him his parachute, as there is in the trust that an individual lost in the jungle extends to a native youth. Trust is courageous, giddy, and lustful.

I

Araouane

*I*T WAS TWO WEEKS BY CAMEL to get to Araouane and
back to Tombouctou; Robin and Ken had to leave Africa
before then. Azima, a Tuareg of twenty-five, arranged for a
vehicle. Azima was born in Araouane; his family lives there.
Unschooled, he speaks fluent French and very good English
and, like most people in Mali, four native languages. The
driver Izzah arrived with a Land Cruiser the next morning.
Dressed also in a Tuareg blue *boubou* with a pale blue turban
of fine fabric on his head, he was a stout middle-aged guy with
perfect teeth and excellent French, energetic and jovial. He
had a lad, Mohammed, with him identified as his mechanic;
during the trip Mohammed also did the cooking. We picked
up a middle-aged, lean, Arab-looking guy, Amadou, always
serious and silent, who was to be the guide.

We drove through the sand roads of Tombouctou and into
desert scattered with thorn trees and tufts of a grass inedible
for camels and goats. The men covered their faces, save for their
eyes, with the ends of their turbans to filter the sandy air. Under
the vacant sky the vehicle growled across dunes and hollows
sometimes white with salt. Now and again there were blackened depressions where water had stood. On a crest the vehicle
got stuck; Mohammed got out and let some air out of the
tires, to increase the area of their traction.

After a few hours, we stopped at a small tree, laid out

3

blankets, and prepared lunch. We had mangoes and dates and dark flat breads. The men cooked lamb and rice over a fire of sticks. I strolled off into the distances. The sands were very fine, yellow beach sand, rippled like the patterns in watered silk. A white mist of salt swirled over the surfaces. Here and there were small fields of black basalt pebbles. The sands were drifting in sheets, eastward to Niger, Chad, Sudan, to eventually silt in the Red Sea.

Walking over the sand gave me a hitherto unknown sensation of walking on the very surface. In the waves of the Sahara that range over three and a half million square miles, I was a water bug gliding across the surface of a pond. Everywhere else I have walked on this earth, I have been shadowed and enveloped by buildings and trees higher than myself. The presence of a dark depth beneath, into which elsewhere the trees sank their taproots and in which the dead are buried, was missing here. One is on sand, and below there is sand. Here I could only be buried in sand and disinterred by the winds.

We reached whole stretches where not a blade of vegetation was visible. The time of human concerns, and that of our own journey, faded out before the presence of geological time, which extended across the crests and hollows drifting under the featureless sky. The horizons that opened unendingly upon flowing desert, the presence of deep water into which occasional desert wells descended, the blackened basins where water still stood during the rains took one back across centuries indistinguishable from one another. We stopped; the men got out, spread blankets across the sand, and once again prostrated themselves in homage to Allah. Over them the empty silences of the sky opened upon cosmic time.

Amadou is directing Izzah across a path that the *azalaï*, the camel caravans of the Tuareg, have taken for a thousand years, each camel bearing four two-hundred-pound slabs of brown salt from the mines at Taoudenni. Yesterday, an hour ago, camels left their hoofprints somewhere in these spaces, but the winds have erased them already. The great dunes that loom up are as ephemeral as the crests of waves in the oceans. Everything is ephemeral in this immemorial time. The tufts of grass visible here and there will be gone in another hour when another camel caravan passes.

Amadou indicates the way with small turns of his hand. Azima and Izzah know the way, but not this well. Izzah says that Amadou has the map in his head, and the invisible paths to Mauritania and Libya and Niger too. The camel caravans travel by night guided by the stars: celestial navigators. When the sky is overcast a Tuareg verifies the way by tasting the sand!

In the late afternoon we have a flat tire. I see a man with a child coming across the emptiness. For his children, sick with fever, he asks for aspirin. Which I had.

At the end of the day we stop to gather some sticks; Izzah tells us there will be no more to be found from now on. He does not seem to care about the approaching dark. Indeed it is soon upon us. For hours I have watched Amadou signal the way across utterly trackless desert; now its dimensions are reduced to a band that the headlights extend into the night. He directs Izzah with precise movements of his hand, peering into the cone of light ahead. He has literally memorized the shapes and spacing of tufts of grass over hundreds of kilometers! I try to project what his mind is doing into my head—in vain. I think that no scholar reading the philosopher Hegel has so exacting an attentiveness to so vast a mental space. Perhaps Ravi Shankar improvising a six-hour raga on the sitar could give an idea of his mind.

About ten o'clock, we are suddenly in Araouane. I can barely make out a few walls in the dark. The people warmly welcome Izzah; they exchange the long litanies of greeting. They lay out blankets and pillows on the sand for us, and we are surrounded by some twenty young men and kids, noisily joking and laughing over us. Then suddenly they all rush off: the mullah is there. He seats himself on the blanket, lays out a small charcoal brazier and kettle, and at length offers us the ritual three glasses of mint tea: the first *bitter as death,* the second *mild like life,* the third *sweet as love.* There is no moon; the stars are dim in the sandy haze of the night. The heat is gone, but the sands envelop us with their balmy warmth and the wind moves clouds of light sand continually over us.

I woke as the black of the sky was thinning into a russet haze. Great dunes surged about us, and, in the hollows, the ten flat banco buildings of Araouane half buried in the sand. The sun rose a pewter disk in ochre mists. Azima brought a kettle of water for us to rinse our faces, crusted with sand. A little girl came to offer us necklaces, one with a piece of amber, the other with five small shells, formerly used as money in the desert. We had tea in the house of the mullah, whom the light showed to be an old man with pale skin—perhaps of Berber ancestry. The room was small; high in the corner there was a shelf with a few books. Sand was deep on the floor. Breakfast was balls of rice and millet—and sand. Outside a dozen small children were learning Koranic texts written on wood paddles.

Araouane is older than Tombouctou; many old banco buildings are buried deep under our feet. Now Araouane, half-way between Tombouctou and the salt mines of Taoudenni, is an overnight camp for the azalaï. But it is also a holy place; mullahs come to study with the resident holy man. The present mullah had done his studies here with the prior resident. Here is Islam as it first appeared in this place, Islam reduced to the Koran, the prayers, the fasts, in the simplicity, the emptiness, the eternity of the sands and the skies. The sacredness is tangible, in the complete absence of anything trivial.

Izzah proposed to take us to Dar-Taleg. This is a nearby ancient town that had been covered by the sands, then revealed by the winds, and, Izzah tells us, in 1962 explored by an archaeological team. They dated it from the third century CE, collected pottery and artifacts, and left. The sands had covered over their work, but left visible on the surface the white ridges of walls of a dozen rather big houses and a mosque, like the diagram for a future city. There is no vegetation; Dar-Taleg's water source had long ago been buried.

We headed back. I marveled to see now how rare was the salt grass and how featureless the hundred kilometers that Amadou had conducted us across last night.

We stopped twice to get water at wells, where herds of camels, goats, and sheep were being watered. The wells are very deep. A leather bag attached to a long rope is dropped into the well, a camel is led a distance the length of the rope to pull out the bag full of water, and a man swings the bag over to the trough and empties it. I admired the flocks of goats and sheep, who stick together in groups, waiting their turn like so many Catholic boarding school classes.

At the second well we bought a sheep; Amadou cut its throat with the knife every Tuareg carries at his waist. I was sickened to see its body long thrash spasmodically the way a decapitated chicken does. When finally it was still, we tied it to the front of the car and set out.

Suddenly the back window shattered—the spare tire had banged against it. Izzah looked around, grinned broadly, and drove on.

In midafternoon we stopped, and Mohammed and Amadou skinned the sheep and cut up a potful of meat, boiling it over a fire of sticks.

We drove on. Then abruptly, crossing a dune indistinguishable from any other, there was Tombouctou, upon which a peaceful desert haze muses.

At Araouane the mullah had a tablet, like those purchased in towns for schoolchildren, in which a few dozen visitors had written their impressions. Soldiers and civil servants wrote florid lines of awe and gratitude for having been able to come here; some tourists had also written their impressions, less eloquent but equally intense. All said that Araouane is a holy place. The sacred is manifest in the decomposition of the arenas of work and reason. The sacred is manifest in the dunes that shift and engulf the houses of Araouane, the winds that spread into them granules of rocks and mountains from far away, carrying off the dust of the banco houses to the trackless distances. The sacred is manifest in the desolation of boundless surfaces spread out under the abysses of the sky.

In fact Araouane had already been a place of power in ancient times of "animism." The sacred is not only the outer spaces, where the world of work and reason dies away. The sacred is also in the past, definitively beyond the designs of work and reason. Before Tombouctou, Araouane was the capital of the Tuareg federation in this region. It is also its great antiquity that makes Araouane a place of pilgrimage today. Like Angkor in Cambodia and Ayutthaya in Thailand, this ancient capital, now reduced to a few houses, has become a holy place.

Great camel caravans from Taoudenni, Marrakesh, and Gao once paused here, rested, and traded. Until quite recently Araouane was a market especially for slaves. Even today the Tuareg keep slaves, *bella,* nominally emancipated in Mali. The market closed down two decades ago. Trucks are relentlessly replacing the camel caravans that Azima still joins, on thirty-two-day journeys each way to bring merchandise from Algeria and Libya to Tombouctou.

The Tuareg, the blue men of the desert, are the great warriors who for ten centuries have been masters of the length and breadth of the Sahara. They became legendary for Europeans, the last and most ferocious resistance to the French, Spanish, and Italian colonial encroachment. During the drought that devastated the Sahel in the eighties, international humanitarian aid was pillaged by the government officials and did not reach the Tuareg, who were most affected by the famine. They entered into rebellion in 1990, and the military government of Mali struck back, destroying nomad camps, poisoning the wells, shooting down camel herds. The people of Araouane fled, the women into tunnels dug in and stabilized under the sands, the men to fight with the rebels. The restless dunes covered their abandoned houses.

Around the fire while the sheep was being roasted, Izzah spoke to us of the depopulation of the region. The great drought of the eighties and the civil war that ended in 1996 destroyed enormous numbers of camels, sheep, and goats. Everybody can see that each year the Sahara is covering with its sands another band of the Sahel denuded of its grasses by the goats. "Our government does nothing!" he said. "But you Americans," he said to me, "you know what to do!" He said an American prospecting team had recently come and begun to search for oil. "Surely, with all the riches Libya derives from oil, there are great resources here!" His gaze turned to the vehicle, which had blown two tires and the rear window. I knew what he was thinking: his expenses would be greater than what he had agreed with us as the price of this trip. He turned back to me and ruefully smiled: "The first thing the Americans will do is lay down a paved road here!"

I was jolted out of my sacred reverie: Araouane would become an oil workers' town, with shacks where tires are vulcanized, stands where trucked-in food is cooked under the blare of television sets; there would be shops. Truck carcasses and garbage would accumulate along its roads; the dunes, like those all around Tombouctou, will be littered with plastic bags. The profane world of work and reason extends only by desecration.

Izzah had stopped five times that day to spread out his blanket over the sands and fervently make his prayer. He has no sense that inviting the American oilmen here is sacrilege. In fact the profane world extends its work and reason without acknowledging its violent compulsion to desecrate. But the compulsion to desecrate is in religion itself. Religion does not create but acknowledges the zone of the sacred, and religion desecrates. Already when Islam came here in the eighth century, the animist gods were driven out of Araouane and the desert was left empty for an Allah to dwell in a transcendent realm above. Is not sacrilege a religious act? It was men serving religion who massacred and burned the ancient gods of Araouane and those of Babylon, Egypt, Constantinople, Tenochtitlán, Qosqo. Temples are built on the ruins of and with the plunder of temples of other religions.

Work and reason are calculation, of benefit and loss. War enlists all the resources of work, reason, and life in a cause of unlimited destruction, where the conquerors are equally delivered over to death and destruction. For it is not only in contemporary war, it was also in the Crusades and the Hundred Years' War, it was in every war, that there are no victors. It is through their thirst for war and conquest that civilizations that perished were destroyed. Religion sends men off to war; every religion blesses and sacralizes war. Religion opens the dimension of the absolute; it absolutizes the always only relative wrongs a people have suffered from another people. Today the Tuareg rebellion continues in Mauritania, Algeria, and Niger.

There is a contemporary horror of desecration, that of postmodern minds in rich postindustrial and multicultural nations. We have come to understand that our future, our wealth, are not in blackened industrial centers but in high-tech miniaturized electronic and information industries. We seek to protect whatever our multiple cultures, and cultures wherever we encounter them, have set aside as sanctuaries. We turn them into information and cultural enrichment— a higher level of desacralization.

I did not hire Izzah to drive me in his Land Cruiser the four days over the sands to reach Mopti. There is an airstrip in Tombouctou. In four hours I was in Bamako, and in another five hours in Paris. Then six hours over the Atlantic to New York. Below there was the trackless ocean, a Sahara of water. I looked out the porthole of the plane into the transparent sky. Our eyes here are relayed by the eyes of astronauts in outer space. We see our own planet from beyond, a blue and green marble in the immensity of cosmic voids. The Hubble tele-scope shows us photographs of the swirling spirals of incandes-cent gases exploding billions of light-years ago. Astronomers measure the number of years yet ahead before the incineration of our planet, the extinction of our sun, the burning out of all the stars of the Milky Way galaxy. Our cosmological and astronomical science has extended the time of the universe beyond the time of our own tasks, of our civilization, of our species. It has reduced to infinitesimal proportions whatever significance we can assign to ourselves in the universe. It opens us upon a cosmic space and time where the end of our species, of our planet, of our sun are marked. To our prag-matic perception of the practicable field about us, our science superimposes a deanthropomorphized and apocalyptic cosmic vision.

Four and a half million years ago the sun hurled out of itself a molten rock, flaming in the dark spaces like a torch heralding destiny. As the surface of the rock cooled, bacteria, along with the fungi and algae entered into symbiotic lichens, proceeded to crumble that rock into sand. We humans con-tinue to decompose the surface of the planet. In the voids of outer space, we can now see the end of the time of work and reason, the end of time. The sacred is manifest in the comets and meteors that crash into planets, in the solar storms, in the extinction of stars grown old and cold. The sacred is manifest in the emptiness of the desert surfaces spread out under an empty sky.

The Song of the Norias

*A*FTER WE CROSSED ISRAEL, where we saw the Holy Land snared with power lines under which factories snarled across weedy plains and bulldozers gouging out rocky hills for new "settlements," a long day's drive northward in Syria brought us at day's end to Hama, where in February 1982 some twelve thousand or more Muslim resisters to the secularizing government were killed.

Here the Orontes River divides and spirals under a high bluff covered with trees. Then it swings in an arc, leaving space under the bluff for the old city. On the side of the river coming in from the plains the city has spread its caravansaries and markets. Ancient mosques, madrassas, covered souks, and hamams await the visitor at every turn. The city has prospered in modern times, and new high-rise apartment buildings now crenellate the upper edge of the basin the river has hollowed out. Beyond are ancient mountains imperceptibly subsiding into the earth, today softened by the late-summer haze.

In the center of the city, where the river loops and divides, we come upon the norias. They are giant waterwheels; one, forty-five feet high, turns on one branch of the river; on the other branch turn a set of three, with heights of thirty-five, forty-five, and fifty feet. Triangular stone bases hold the wood-block seating that supports their central axles. The waterwheels are of wood, black and gleaming with spray. Their spokes are not, like those of a bicycle wheel, inserted into the axle, but fastened across it so that they do not radiate from the axle center but whorl about it. Hundreds of blades set in the rims turn with the flow of the current. The rims are made of hundreds of small wooden boxes; the top of each is open and set with a wood lip such that when it reaches the top it pours its water into the trough of a stone aqueduct whose arcades dance—the one into the old city, the other into its commercial extension.

In a nearby shop we find a little brochure a local historian has printed. We learn that Hama was founded five thousand years ago. The first known mention of norias is a picture in a mosaic that dates from the fifth century CE. There were once a hundred of them along the river; there are still dozens. These in the city center were built in the fourteenth century.

As the norias lift the current of the river their axles sing. A rich bass tone rises and descends across a narrow range, enriched with overtones from the sounding-boxes of the spokes. The larger wheels turn more slowly and sing a deeper song. The set of three wheels sing a chord, joined by the song of the single wheel on the other branch of the river. The spray of the water, on which rainbows hover, improvises fleeting grace notes around the song of the norias. It's a contemplative song, and once your ears catch on to it you continue to hear it through the bustle of the crowds and the traffic of the city.

Five times a day the muezzins mount the steps of the minarets of the city's mosques and intone the soaring cadences of the *Allah u-akbar!* heard all over Islam, from Morocco to Mindanao, the fourteen-hundred-year-old song of the world to the skies. The norias accompany them with their basso continuo, and continue to sing when the voices are stilled.

In India there are tones called mantras, cosmic sounds that the human voice picks up and sends outward again, but especially draws inward, until finally they are no longer voiced but reverberate within, centering and bringing harmony to all the turbulent voices of the body.

In Edirne, which the Ottomans had made their capital for eighty years as they surrounded and laid siege to Constantinople, I had gone to see the first mosque built by the great architect Sinan, who later crowned Istanbul with its Sultan Ahmet and Süleymaniye mosques. A mosque, unlike a church, is not a sanctuary, a sacred place; one's prayers said on a mat laid out on the desert sands are as holy. It is not building a grandiose prayer hall that is meritorious, but building the complex about it: the school, the hospital, the shelters for widows and orphans and the deranged, lodging for travelers, and the dispensaries of food and clothing for the poor. The prayer hall in Edirne is small; what enchants the eye is the symmetrical complex of colonnades and domed buildings for works of mercy that surround the garden and its central fountain. I was especially intrigued by the section, immediately adjacent to the prayer hall, that Sinan designed for the insane. Each person had a large individual room whose fifteen-foot-high stone walls kept it cool and whose stained-glass windows kept a dawn light glowing under its high dome. Since these people were disturbed, the rooms did not communicate with one another but instead into a central courtyard. The donor who supplied the funds for the mosque complex must also ensure that it be supported in perpetuity; this was typically done by building an adjacent market where merchants would be taxed to support the works of the mosque. Thus we have documents where all the details of the operations of the complex were specified. And so we know that the therapy for the patients of the asylum at Edirne consisted in music: an orchestra played each day in the courtyard music to harmonize the soul; by night the fountain continued its melodies. For seven hundred years, until World War I put an end to the Ottoman Empire and the people fled the mosque complex and Edirne was mostly destroyed during the Turkish-Greek war, this music sounded in the asylum.

In Hama I sat in the garden at night and received the mantra of the norias. In the moonlight the whorls of the spokes turned;

my eyes did not stray from them. The wall of the aqueduct behind rose and descended rhythmically. Hours passed.

Genesis begins: the Spirit moved over the waters. More exactly, water is the spirit of the earth; it is visible only by welcoming the sunlight, moonlight, and starlight in all its depth; restless, pure and purifying, it moves with a gentle but determined force. Solar explosion created the planet; water has created life on it.

One is dumbstruck by the ingenuity of the human mind that contrived the waterwheel. Unlike machines, it is not fabricated for the production of things whose purposes only denatured human animals could conceive. The norias are made of wood from trees the river has grown, set in a triangle of stones the rains have found and exposed to the light. They lift and pour water with the movement of the river. They do not reverse the movement of the river, for of itself water rises to the sky and descends again in rain. The water the norias lift flows forth into the trough of the aqueduct to flow gently down into the gardens and wells of the old city.

Those who cut the timber and built the norias did not intend to create their song, did not create their song. They themselves were astonished when they heard the song that like a mantra the trees had sung inwardly for so long. Today, seven hundred years later, the people of Hama gather each evening in the gardens about the banks of the river and hear the song.

Facades

*Y*OU SEE IT. Looking at a topological map, you see
this gaping crack in the continent—what unflappable
Victorian gave it the innocuous name of the Great Rift Valley?
Thirty kilometers east of Nairobi, you see how the high plateau
is split apart; you look down cliff walls so steep that finally it
was German prisoners of war who were forced to blast a road
down them. On a clear day you make out the vertical walls
of the other side. From the bottom Mount Kilimanjaro and
Mount Kenya sizzled up in volcanic eruptions to their glacier-
covered heights. When you get to the bottom you can see the
gorges where the Leakeys found bones of the earliest hominids.
This was the Garden of Eden where human apes first stood
upright.

Farther north the Great Rift Valley cuts through the high
mountain stronghold of Ethiopia. There archaeologist Donald
Johnson found the first quasi-complete skeleton of the human
ape he and his co-workers, in a hallucinogenic vision, named
Lucy—Lucy in the Sky with Diamonds.

Still farther north you see the great fracture filled with water
named the Gulf of Aqaba; with only a narrow strait opening
upon the Red Sea on its south end, its waters are twice as salty as
the ocean. Then farther up, the Dead Sea (whose greatest depth
at 1,312 feet below sea level is the lowest point on Earth's surface), and further up still the Sea of Galilee. Between the Gulf

of Aqaba and the Dead Sea a tectonic compression gradually lifting great strata of sandstone and porphyry finally blocked the Jordan River, and the life of the Dead Sea was choked in the ever-increasing concentrations of bromine, magnesium, iodine, and salt. Some hundred kilometers south of the Dead Sea the surface now rose in mountains to 3,280 feet.

At the place now called Petra, just south of this high point, an earthquake thirty million years ago split the rock in a zig-zag fissure called Siq. You see that countless flash floods of the Wadi Mousa have since carved it to a width of five to ten feet. You enter it between vertical walls three to six hundred feet high that reveal the swirling strata of rock, some but a fraction of an inch thick, tinted in alternations of ochres, reds, blacks, purples, blues. Where the sun breaks through, bright green fig trees cling to the rock walls, offering their fruits to you as to travelers long ago. Looking up you see the whorls of rock perforated with inner channels that the artistry of torrential waters has carved, a gallery of sculpture styles and fashions favored by the succeeding generations of flash floods. (Immanuel Kant looked at pages written by David Hume and declared that we never see causality, that causality is just an organizational device of the rational mind. How myopic was that transcendental lucidity of modern philosophy!)

A kilometer down, abruptly, at a bend, your astonished eyes see that another artistry has carved in the wall of the gorge a great facade: six pillars, and above them a tholos, a round templet, whose conical roof is topped by an urn, with pillared semipediments on either side, the whole adorned with now defaced sculptures of eagles, amazons, lions, and gods in high relief. There is but a small room behind, square and unadorned. You learn that experts cannot decide whether it was a tomb, a memorial mausoleum, or a temple; they still call it the Bedouin name: the Treasury. You walk on; the gorge widens, narrows and turns, then opens wide between mountainous heights where you see hundreds of carved caves: dwellings and tombs.

In a bend, surrounded by tombs on both sides and above, you see hollowed out the perfect half circle of a vast theater. On your right you see the mountain wall carved with what looks like the facades of buildings, each different, up to a hundred fifty feet high. Your eyes climb three colonnaded ramps, then back to the recessed columns before a high wall sliding up the mountain. Your gaze lingers over a facade whose columns and cornices have melted; the polychrome striations of the rock have turned into wild shot silk. Your look wanders among the four stories of colonnades of a majestic facade that turn the Jebel el-Khubtha mountain behind into a palace. You have entered the city its creators called Reqem.

They wrote an Aramaic language, so we know they were called Nabateans. Their first king was named Aretas I; he assumed power about 168 BCE. Their rule extended from Damascus to the Gulf of Aqaba, over the Negev, Sinai, and Transjordan and down the Arabian Peninsula to Hegra. Thus they controlled trade from Syria to Yemen, from the Nile to the Tigris and Euphrates, and from India and via the Silk Road from China. Reqem, accessible only through narrow gorges, was their capital.

Farther on, where the mountains are split farthest apart, you see where the city was built. At the widest point three rivers were conducted by way of tunnels and covered channels to gush forth from a gigantic sculptured fountain. A central avenue paved with granite blocks led to the major temples on either side of the fountain; today oleanders, aloes, and junipers perfume their ruins. On one side you see the remains of an immense colonnaded market where caravans laid out their spices, jewels, ivories, and silks from Egypt, Syria, Mesopotamia, Persia, India, and China. About the market the Nabateans erected their homes. Archaeologists estimate the city had a population of thirty to forty thousand.

The most grandiose structures are not buildings but facades carved on the cliff faces. All that there is to them is spread out before the eyes. Behind them there are cubical unadorned rooms of only modest dimensions; one of the grandest facades has no room cut behind it. Nabatean travelers brought back to Reqem in their mind's eye the recollection of all the splendid forms they had seen in the public monuments of great cities from far away. Assyrian, Egyptian, Syrian, Hellenistic, and Roman tectonic structures, columns, entablatures, and architraves, devised to hold up the massive weight of walls over doors and roofs over places of assembly, were here used merely to shape facades on the mountains, snares for the eyes. Opposite the mountain wall they had carved with royal facades, they carved a great semicircular theater with a capacity for seven thousand, where people watched spectacular representations of their own lives. Like that of the Javanese studied by Clifford Geertz,[1] theirs was a theater-state.

You climb the processional stairways, ten feet wide, that they carved up the craggy mountains to sanctuaries on the summits. A mile-long flight of steps brings you to the greatest of these, which the Bedouin call the ad-Deir, the Monastery. It is but a facade—of a tomb, memorial mausoleum, ritual hall, or shrine of a religious order?—its powerful and majestic forms as crisp as if fresh from the chisel, astonishingly not eroded or weather-stained by its two thousand years on this height.

The eleventh and last Nabatean king was Rabbel II, 70–106 CE. The Roman troops were now masters of Syria, Judea, and Egypt; Rabbel II abandoned Reqem and transferred his capital to Bozrah in the north. In 106 Emperor Trajan annexed what was left of Rabbel II's kingdom to the imperial province of Arabia. When the Roman capital was transferred to Byzantium, some small rooms behind the great facades of Reqem were enlarged and turned into Christian churches. An earthquake in 363 and a more severe one in 551 depopulated much of the city. The Arabs conquered the region in 663. By then the great caravans had found other routes and no longer passed through Reqem. The Crusaders occupied and fortified the site briefly

in the twelfth century. As the centuries passed, the site no longer contained an urban population; Bedouin herdsmen have
come to take shelter in its cave tombs. From the departure of
the Crusaders, defeated by Salah ad-Din in 1189, until 1812
when adventurer Johann Ludwig Burckhardt disguised himself as a Koranic scholar to pass through the gorge and told of
it in his posthumous *Travels in Arabia,* memory of Reqem had
been lost in the West. Since 1842, when Scottish artist David
Roberts published his drawings, people have come to see.

When you come and see, you think, This is what our eyes
were made to see! For our sight is not turned to ourselves, our
look sees nothing of our eyes, so little of our body. Eyes are
enfeebled and imprisoned when fixed to the tools and obsta-
cles at hand, to what can be possessed. This distance sense is
made for the remote things, the grand things; eyes are visionary. You wander the gorge; your gaze springs forth into the
radiant transparency opened indefinitely toward outer spaces
by the sun. Your look leaps forth from you unto the walls of
the gorge, seeking the rock, seeking the swirling colors of the
rock strata, seeking the facades cut into the walls of the gorge
by the Nabateans, making them visions. Your look does not
bound back to you, does not extract anything from them for
you. Before this epiphany you lose sight of yourself, you are
this ecstasy of vision.

   You realize that this transport of vision was what you had
not found in the cities you had gone to, looking at the churches,
mosques, and temples they had to show you. Set apart from
all profane uses, they claimed to be sacred places, places where
the transcendent opens. But how much of man your eyes saw
there! The Parthenon, which uses the chthonic force of the
Acropolis rock to elevate for all to see a construction only a
human geometer could contrive, housed Athena, deified figure
of the Athenian state. How logical that the Persians would
destroy it. In the gods of feudal cathedrals you saw kings

and queens. The silver cities of Mexico are overfull of gilded churches whose side chapels are mausoleums of robber barons. Myanmar is overfull of temples; rich people are garnering merit for their next reincarnation, but especially monumental-izing their ambition, in building yet another.

Looking at these churches, mosques, and temples, modern humans have finally convinced themselves that it is the human spirit that creates splendor out of what are only colors, sounds, shapes, and material substances. Artistry is seated in the human soul. It requires freedom, the freedom to depart from what is given and to create; it exists only in human animals. Humans even convinced themselves that the recognition of beauty exists only in human animals (contriving utilitarian explana-tions for the plumage of hummingbirds and for the designs of coral fish).

But when the human apes first descended from the trees they stood erect by holding on to the trees until their torsos themselves became trunks, and it was the winds and the birds that taught them to sing and to sing with the voices of the winds and the birds. And it was the winds and the rivers that taught the Nabateans to carve the stone. Caves designed by the river showed them dwellings for their dead and their gods. Everywhere vertical cracks divide the cliffs into blocks; these the Nabateans took as units for their carvings. The dozens of facades they carved into the wrinkled and pitted flanks of the mountains revealed swirling melodies of rose, salmon, ochre, saffron, aquamarine, and violet in the rock. They did not clear the chaos of the mountain surfaces around them; their most magnificently proportioned facade is that of the ad-Deir, set on a summit; in order to see it, you have to spiral your way up the mountain whose cliffs and outcroppings pour down stalac-tites like a petrified fountain.

Emperor Hadrian visited Reqem in 130 and renamed it Petra Hadriane—and Petra is the name that modern Roma-centric historians and the Jordan Ministry of Tourism literature still call it. Yet the name is the right one, for here the artist compulsion moves in the stone itself.

On the summits and in the gorges, the Nabateans revered the great spirit Dushara, he who separates night and day; al-ʿUzza, goddess of love and of fortune; At-Kutba, spirit of commerce and inscription; and al-Qaum, spirit of caravans. These supreme forces of the earth were aniconic, represented only as blocks of stone in the form of a truncated pyramid, cube, parallelepiped, cylinder, or hemisphere.

In the fourth century BCE Hieronymus of Cardia described the Nabateans as nomads who ranged their camels and sheep over the desert, neither planting grain nor setting out fruit-bearing trees nor constructing houses. Then the Wadi Mousa gorge captivated them, and for three centuries they built their city and carved the mountain walls. In the centuries since the Arab conquest of 663, Bedouin have inhabited the caves and tombs of the old Nabatean capital during the cold winter months, moving their herds to higher pastures during the long hot season.

Already a band of forty Christian monks led by Bar Sauma had destroyed the statues of the temples of Petra in 423; now Muslim iconoclasts have defaced the figures carved in relief on the facades. Many of them have been obliterated recently, since the visit of David Roberts, who drew them in 1839.

Yet Petra was for the Bedouin a preternatural place. Nearby is the Ain Mousa spring, which, according to the Bible, Moses had caused to flow by striking a rock with his rod; it flows still. Petra, the Bedouin held, was created by the great pharaoh who pursued Moses out of Egypt, created as a storehouse for his fabulous riches, which were deposited here by magic. The nineteenth-century Westerners who tried to penetrate the city were fiercely repelled by the Bedouin, who suspected them of being magicians who had come to reclaim the wealth of the Pharaoh. Burckhardt wrote, "They believe that it is sufficient

for a true magician to have seen and observed the spot where
the treasures are hidden . . . in order to be able afterwards, at
his ease, to command the guardian of the treasure to set the
whole before him."[2] Today you see the goddess at the top of the
great facade in the Siq riddled by bullets from Bedouin who
hoped to strike the spot from which the treasure would pour.

In the early 1980s the Jordanian government decided to
turn Petra into an archaeological and tourist area—the Petra
National Park. They relocated the Bedouin in a village outside built for them. Archaeologists and historians set out to
supply an understanding of what, for the visitor, is a spectacle
for the pure ecstasy of vision. Comparative archaeologists
explained that Assyrian, Egyptian, Syrian, Hellenistic, and
finally Roman architectural elements were shaped here, in
this crossroads of caravan routes, into distinctive ensembles.
Unlike other Semitic kingdoms, unlike neighboring Judea, the
Nabatean kingdom was not subordinated to a ruling religious
ideology. The Nabateans later syncretized Zeus, Dionysus,
Osiris, and Serapis with their Dushara; Aphrodite, Tyche, and
Isis with their al-ʿUzza. As they labored to uncover the debris
with which earthquakes and floods had covered the ancient
city, the archaeologists and historians dug back through the
pharaonic legends and long memories of their own histories
there with which Bedouin had covered every site. They only
succeed in replacing Bedouin legends with their own speculations. From the start they assumed that the great facades of the
west wall were royal tombs, but were able to assign the name
of a king to not one of them. For most they have not been able
to this day to decide if they were tombs, funereal mausoleums,
temples, or ritual banquet halls.

Out of classifications of the origins of coins, legends on
coins and rare inscriptions in stone, and rare mention of the
Nabateans by (always partisan) Greek and Jewish writers, the
researchers then provide a text for the spectacle. It is all about
the names, the kings and queens, the caravan routes. One will

say that this kind of text functions to fill in a gap in the text of scientific universal history. But can any history of humans be knowledge for the sake of knowledge? Is not every history written for the present generation, used for its political, economic, and social enterprises? Whatever the archaeologists and historians determine is popularized in tourist guides. Petra today is for the Jordanian Ministry of Tourism its most important draw. One imposing monumental tomb in exceptional condition has a luxury hotel built over it, and the tomb itself has been outfitted as the hotel bar.

And for those of us who come to see Petra, these texts, these speculations about the kings and the queens and the mercantile empire, function as a screen set in front of our eyes—as the anecdotes about an author function to dissipate the spell of an epic poem, as psychobiographies about the composer function to level the transcendent soarings of Beethoven's *Missa Solemnis.* For what Petra has to offer is what our visionary eyes are made for: the ecstasy of vision.

The city of the living, the homes and workshops and markets, erected on the valley floor crumbled and were covered with rubble and sand centuries ago; what you see mainly are what experts have identified as tombs cut in the mountain walls and the colossal "royal" facades taken to be tombs or shrines for funereal rituals—entries to the realm of the dead. The great semicircular theater was carved down in the midst of banks of tombs. "Strange contrast!" wrote the American theologian Edward Robinson in 1838, "where a taste for the frivolities of the day was at the same time gratified by the magnificence of tombs; amusement in a cemetery; a theater in the midst of sepulchers."[3] All that remains visible then is evidence of the invisible.

How incomprehensible to us has become this belief, seemingly as old as humankind, that a decomposing cadaver will leap integral and alive again into another world! How strange that peoples of Egypt and Arabia, who daily see animals of every species die and their corpses devoured or turn into decay and filth, could have acted on a belief in the resurrection of human bodies with the inestimable labor that went into the Egyptian pyramids, into all these facades here! We think that once our cadaver is put into the rock of tombs, it will disintegrate into the minerals from which it too is composed. Our eyes that are so imperiously, so ecstatically drawn to the rock have an intimation of the destination of our lives, not to another kingdom of life, but to this rock.

We are pragmatic; what we know, Martin Heidegger said, is what we can work out; for us to know what things are is to see how they work. Yet is not our extinction unthinkable? When someone we know dies, we weep: it is impossible that she should be dead. We say over and over again, I can't believe it.

We are positivist. Everything we know in our advanced biological sciences about our organism convinces us that once its neurological substrate is destroyed, our conscious life will be annihilated. But once we try to think this nothingness, try to think, In ten years, in ten days, I will be *nothing,* we find the mind cannot think this thought, cannot endure trying to think this thought.

We look at the gigantic funereal facades so laboriously carved to such perfection by the Nabateans, facades behind which there are no rooms or passageways, only the immense darkness of inert rock, and our vision is held on a surface behind which there is the unthinkable.

The winds continue to erode the two-thousand-year-old sculptured facades; flash floods wear away the bases of the monuments. In 1896 another earthquake broke up many structures; in 1967 a flash flood in the Siq drowned a group of tourists. The hot sun and the snowy winters are fissuring the mountain surfaces. The winds and water are turning the precision-cut lines of the facades into abstract works of art.

Even if the scientists will one day decide to spray some protective coat on the sandstone mountains, eventually the winds, water, and sun will have effaced the last trace of human intention from the great gorge. The mountains will pursue their delirious artistry.

Unknowable Intelligence

*T*HE DAY I ARRIVED IN LIMA the sun shone weakly for two hours. The next day there was sunshine for only an hour, the day after none at all. The *garúa* had set in, that strange cold ocean fog that covers the Peruvian coast for four months. As the weeks went by the fog became more dense, saturated with the city's traffic and industrial pollutants. In my room my clothes were damp and my papers limp; outside buildings were wet and the streets muddy, though there was no rain. Now for even short distances I took taxis, antiquated contraptions that stall at red lights and only keep on the streets by cannibalizing parts of those taxis that have expired. I had to escape; I decided to go to Nazca.

I took a taxi to the airport and waited at a pillar that had been designated for me. Soon the pilot appeared, Carlos, a mustached youth with dark glasses and a smart brown pilot's jacket. He led me out a back door and to the far end of the runway, to a Cessna. He seated and buckled me alongside him. The Cessna lifted and pitched into the garúa and then leveled above it. Here was the sun, glorious and sovereign, that I had not seen for months! Seen now from above, the garúa was an immaculate lamb's-wool blanket that extended uninterrupted and featureless over the ocean to our right; far to our left from time to time glacier-covered peaks of the Andes broke through it like a syncopation in that whiteness. It was

31

impossible to situate myself any longer in relation to Lima
and its dark wet streets, impossible to locate myself on any
coordinates marked by roads, cities, continents; planet Earth
had veered off and continued its way without us. For three
hours the Cessna, untroubled by any turbulence, seemed not
to move, poised in this solar space without markers.

Then Carlos turned the nose of the Cessna gently down-
ward and the lamb's wool rose about it and then began to thin.
And I began to see long pale lines in the white fog, elongated
triangles, quadrangles, and trapezoids. A few minutes later as
the fog lifted off them they stabilized on the gray plain below.
Carlos now leveled the Cessna and circled back and forth over
the coastal plain, where the lines spread in rays for, he said,
130 kilometers, heading off in all directions, hundreds of them,
many intersecting one another. He pointed out here and there
lines that spiraled and turned into a condor, a frigate bird, a
hawk, a hummingbird, a parrot, a huge bird with a zigzag neck
longer than its body. He said that there were eighteen birds. He
turned the plane to show me a monkey, two llamas, a dog, a
crocodile, an orca, a fish, an iguana, a spider, a flower, and then,
on the flank of the first mountain of the Andes, the figure of a
man with a circle for a head, which Carlos called the owl-man.

Finally we landed. Now I could see that the lines are very
shallow, most only a few centimeters deep. The plain of fine
pebbles, once under the ocean, has trace gypsum in it that
holds the lines fixed. No sands have covered them nor has erosion smeared them. This region is the most arid place known
on the planet; rain is rarer here than in the Sahara. The rare
land traveler who since Pizarro's conquest passed by them
assumed they were remains of ancient irrigation systems. The
lines form diagrams so large—up to twelve hundred meters
long—and the terrain is so flat that someone standing in the
midst of them could not see the patterns. In the thirties they
built the Pan-American Highway across them. Over this coastal
plain the cold Humboldt Current coming from the Antarctic

spreads a dense sea fog. Finally in 1932, Carlos told me, a pilot
was flying a small plane under the fog and noticed that instead
of forming the grid of an irrigation system, they formed strange
geometrical diagrams.

We headed to the small cottage where Maria Reiche lives.
On her veranda we had tea and some lunch. In 1932, as a young
German mathematician working on her doctorate, she was
spending her summer vacation in Qosqo. For a pastime she
was looking into the astronomical mathematics of the Inca
civilization. She met the pilot and then went to see the lines at
Nazca. She started to map them, using surveying instruments
and charting them on a scale of 1 centimeter = 10 meters. One
day she was astonished to see that she was drawing a giant
hummingbird. She never left Nazca. By carbon-dating some
wood posts she has determined that the lines were drawn from
300 BCE to 900 CE, sometimes over previously drawn lines.
Most of them are geometrical figures—zigzags, rays, oscillating
lines, elongated triangles, quadrangles, bent trapezoids, spirals,
double spirals, stars. They are found on vast plains, narrow
plateaus between gorges, and on islands of even ground amid
a maze of dry ancient riverbeds. They are drawn with astonishing precision—lines extending 2,600 feet deviate from the perfectly straight by but 2 inches. Those that depict the animals
and the man that Carlos had shown me from the air are each
made with one continuous line that never crosses over itself.

They were made by a people whose culture had disappeared
long before the Inca extended their rule from Qosqo and Quito
in the high Andes. The Nazca civilization had been one of
great technological and artistic achievements, with splendid
weaving—a piece of fabric was found with 750 threads per
square centimeter, a world record—and some of the finest pottery of ancient Peru. But the lines themselves were their sole
inscription. They, the greatest text or artwork ever created on
our planet, lay in the fog of mystery.

One day, on the equinox, a friend of Maria Reiche's noticed

that one of the major lines headed straight to the horizon where the sun was setting. It gave her her first clue. The lines form, she hypothesized, a gigantic cosmic map. The figures of condors, hummingbirds, and monkeys represent constellations. It is a hypothesis she is still working to verify. She has been able to coordinate only a small number of the lines with the night sky. All of her identifications are subject to question: since the earth wobbles on its axis over time, to determine that that line marked the setting sun on the day of the equinox one would have to know when it was drawn. But the lines were drawn over a twelve-hundred-year period. Others have tried other hypotheses. Anthropologists are convinced they must have religious significance: the exactness of the lines, drawn perfectly straight over many miles and over so many centuries, demonstrates that the lines had transcendent importance. Since the pictorial figures are made with one continuous line that never intersects with itself, may they not be paths for ritual processions? Yet major lines do not lead to any cave or spring that might have had sacred significance but instead just come to a stop in the empty plain. In places free of lines there are circles of ashes, but no trace of bones from possible sacrifices were found in them. Some of the lines continue to the foothills of the Andes and then go straight up, marking a supposed path no human could climb. The recent observation that almost all the lines drawn converge upon some sixty-two ray centers made anthropologists recall that forty-one lines radiated out from the Sun Temple of Qosqo, built five hundred years after the disappearance of the Nazca culture. On those lines there were marked 328 sacred points signifying elements from many levels of Inca thought—from cosmology, astronomy, natural phenomena, irrigation, kinship, social hierarchy, ancestors, and state ideology. Did so many levels of thought also enter into the drawings at Nazca?

The fact that the diagrams are so huge and the terrain so flat that the people who made them could never have seen them is deeply puzzling. The Nazca people must have proceeded as Maria Reiche did when she drew her map of them, but in reverse, translating one centimeter into ten meters. The fact that they could not have seen the figures they drew gave rise to speculations that they were drawn for awaited or real alien visitors. The figure drawn ninety-eight feet high on the mountain, the one Carlos had called the owl-man, looks like a cartoon alien.

For more than fifty years Maria Reiche studied these hypotheses and others, and she continues her research into astronomical mathematics. Now suffering severe arthritis and in her nineties, Maria Reiche conceded to us that on her bad nights she thinks we may never decipher them.

Carlos and I went back to the Cessna and glided over the lines once more. Then the Cessna rose again into the somber fog and emerged from its radiant top surface. Carlos told me that recently he brought here a man who, it turned out, pilots a hot air balloon in his country. When this man saw a piece of Nazca weaving, it occurred to him that fabric woven so fine would not allow air to pass through it—the fabric of hot air balloons is not woven so fine. Perhaps the Nazca people observed their millennial artistry from hot air balloons. That would explain those circles of ashes that were found in flat empty places on the plain and in which the anthropologists could identify no traces of human habitation or sacrifice.

Back in Lima, I picked up *Time* magazine in the airport and found that it contained a special report on the astonishing data supplied by the Hubble Space Telescope, including the first photographs of stars in the process of forming. I was staggered, thinking of how our small animal brains have been able to comprehend the inner processes of inert matter, even at the remote ends of the universe and back during the first milliseconds of the Big Bang. Yet at Nazca the thought behind these lines, not squiggles of disturbed minds sometimes seen in our mental hospitals, but a project executed with exacting precision and over twelve centuries by an advanced human civilization that came to an end not that long ago—fifteen hundred years after Greece, whose philosophers we quite understand—may remain definitively irrecoverable and lost to us.

Rings

*T*HERE WAS THEN A TIME when nothing had meaning. The time when, as an infant, we reached out to kiss our mother or to suckle her breast, to make contact with what was being offered us or what we saw at a distance, or we covered our face, pushed our hand back from what touched us. From a few days old, when we started smiling, our body was animated with "expressions"—grins, grimaces, pouts, frowns, cries, hand-waving, and soon dances and an astonishing gamut of vocalizations. These do not express meanings conceived inwardly; they anticipate contacts our body will make, go back to embraces our body has already made and no longer makes, slow down the couplings our body is making with things and events or accelerate them, detach them or unite them, map them out or segment them. Our fights are in this sense "expressive." Today too; an argument gets *settled* with a fight. Especially an argument about our courage, our honor, our loyalty, or the sincerity and strength of our love.

Soon we used sounds to refer to things, first to joyously acknowledge, or to demand, their being given or taken away, then to acknowledge or demand details. Then we learned words; they designated meanings taken from things and we used words in the absence of those things. Each word refers laterally to a constellation of other words with whose meanings its meaning contrasts: a fork is not a spoon or a knife; each of those words refers to further constellations: don't play with that fork, you'll hurt yourself. It is the ring of words about this word that determines its meaning, and the rings of words about each of them that explain their meanings. This increasingly articulated system of words and their meanings extends a chain-link fence between us and the forces of things, plants, and animals.[1]

It was not all by ourselves that we started asking, What does it mean? and entered into these circles upon circles of interpretation. After all, we do not ask ourselves what it means that we have oatmeal with strawberries for breakfast, that we sink into a hot tub for a half hour when we get back from work; we do not ask ourselves what it means that humans eat breakfast, that humans eat, that humans immerse themselves in warm water—unless, of course, a psychoanalyst faces us to ask, What does that say about you? As little children we were allowed to suck on our thumbs, play for hours with a puppy, run again and again through piles of autumn leaves, without having to worry about what it all meant.

But then they started. Our parents, our teachers faced us and demanded that we give an account of what we did. Now the social worker turns up, and asks, What is the meaning of this new big-screen television in your house, since you are on welfare? Every time we turn on the television there are those faces: senators and pundits demanding what it means that we do not vote, experts demanding what it means that we parents are not disciplining our children, preachers demanding what it means that we don't seem to care that no real meaning can be assigned to our lives, to human life on Earth. Week after week newsmagazines ask what it means that high school kids are shooting down their comrades in school, that people are buying more and more cellular phones, that the hit film of the year is *Fight Club*.

Whenever we wonder, What does this mean? we get caught up in these rings interlocked endlessly upon rings. In another land we have a conversation with someone and then a dinner

together. In this place where no one knows us we abandon
ourselves to the longings and pleasures of lovemaking. It
happens again the next night and the night after that. Then
questions start up in our head: Is she really drawn to me? Is
she playing some sort of game with me? Is she faking orgasm?
Does she expect presents, money, does she want to tie me to
her so that I will bring her to America? Does she want to trap
me by getting pregnant? Everything she does becomes a sign
to be interpreted—every phrase, every sigh or gasp in lovemaking, whether she comes early or comes late, whether she
dresses up or dresses down. Then we find ourselves shifting
into another cycle of questions: Is she aiming for some kind of
triumph in seducing a white man, one of the colonial race? Is
it because the GIs were here during the Vietnam War that the
local morality broke down and women started going to bed
with foreign strangers? Then: What do her parents think of
her and of me, what does her society think? Are they simply
Buddhists free from Judeo-Christian hang-ups about sex?
Or is it the breakdown of their society under the pressure of
Western world-market consumerism that makes her willing to
go to bed with me—something that women back home do not
do? Another circle. And what about me? Is this a serious affair,
which I will have to explain to my wife when I get back? Or
is it a secret affair that means something only to me? Another
circle. What does it mean in my life that I am having an affair, far from my wife? How does this affect my conception
of myself, my status as a married man? Another circle. What
will it mean when I go back to my post as a university professor, will I miss this detour into exoticism? What will it mean
when I teach ethics to young people, I who am indulging in
this secret double life? Another circle. The way we respond to
the question, What does it mean? is to say: the fact that she is
late means that I am not the center of her life; she has a double
life. The fact that I am having an affair means that I am being
unfaithful to my wife and children. The interpretation opens

upon the question what a double life means, what infidelity means. We find ourselves in a realm where there are no facts, only interpretations of interpretations. Infidelity means violating my marriage vows to my wife. But what does marriage really mean? And what does having a wife, what does saying "my wife" mean?

These questions do not arise spontaneously, as though for us to live is to itemize the meaning of everything we see and touch. The question, Does she want to get something from me, does she expect presents, money; does she want to tie me to her? anticipates the time when we will be leaving and she will face us and ask us to take her to America. The question, Is it because the GIs were here during the Vietnam War that the local morality broke down and women started going to bed with foreign strangers? anticipates the time when someone back home with political and ethical convictions will call us to account for what we were doing with that woman in a backward country. The question, What does it mean in my life that I am having an affair, far from my wife? anticipates some friend back home, or some marriage counselor or pastor, some prosecutor who will demand an accounting of us.

Travel far enough and we find ourselves happily back in the infantile world. In Antarctica our gaze is captivated by contours and crevices in the ice sheets, forms and facets in the cliffs for which we can attach no concepts, not even identify by the names of geometrical forms. The sun streaks colors in the ice that we amuse ourselves trying to name: azure, mauve, sodium, cerulean, amethyst, jade, emerald, violet, lavender, lime, absinthe, quetzal—but all these names of blues and greens that we saw in liquid, mineral, plant, and animal substances do not match these gleams in the crystal cliffs. There is nothing here we can link as means to ends; The Ice is a continent we cannot inhabit. Wandering in the deserts of southern Ethiopia, our eyes pass through the encrusted layer of concepts, categories, and explanatory paradigms in our brain and we see again camels, people, dunes, and skies as we did before meanings got spread over everything.

Ken has been traveling since he finished college. Then he took stock of the fact that he would need a job to keep on traveling. He went to graduate school and got a post in academia because academics get more time off you can spend traveling than anybody else except press stringers and writers of airport potboilers. Ken has the kind of health and endurance that can go anywhere. He is big, broad-shouldered; he has built powerful, competition-class muscles. Muscles that are pointless in a university professor who needs only strength enough to turn the pages of a book, tap on a computer, and lift a glass of cheap wine at departmental socials. In Israel and in Syria people asked him if he was in the army. But Ken disdains musculature built to be put to use; he wants to be a freak. He never played football in high school. He has big, wide-set green eyes, candid, without guile or irony, like those of a child. They are incessantly warmed with pleasure, with appetite for all he sees. He is not stocking up on things. Wherever he goes he writes no essays or diaries, takes no pictures.

Ken was once engaged to be married, and bought rings, handmade silver rings he found in Mexico. He dropped out of the engagement, but kept his ring. He likes it, crafted by jewelers from the scraps still found in what were once the richest silver mines in the world. His parents were disappointed; they had liked her.

The other primates in Africa form bands bound together by a basic intraspecies attraction, affection, and sexual interest, as well as for defense. Human societies are formed inasmuch as humans are interdependent on one another in the regulated exchange of goods and services. The recognition of promises, obligations, and debts in the market is the basis for all subsequent development of societies governed by internal laws. We no longer pledge our commercial commitments with a handshake; we use our hands to write our signature on a contract.

But we secure our commitment in marriage on our hand;
a wedding ring shows that the marriage contract binds our
bodies together as with metal loops that cannot be opened.
An engagement or a wedding ring encircles our finger tightly,
and the last of our taboos prevents it from being removed in
the workplace, street, or bar in a convention hotel.

Just now three women are in love with Ken; he lives with
one, travels with another, and visits the third. Every month
or two he meets another woman and falls in love. His grand-
father is ailing; his parents have let Ken know that the old
man wants to see his grandchild, inevitable anyway one day,
before he dies. Ken took off for Ethiopia.

I agreed to join him. He got there first and found a hotel
in Addis Ababa. Waiting for me, he went down to the hotel's
office to e-mail his girlfriends. When I got there I saw that the
young woman in the office could not take her eyes off him.
Ken would disappear in the e-mail room several hours a day.

What did we know of Ethiopia? The Semitic peoples of
Ethiopia had occupied the high mountainous plateau, the
greatest altitudes in Africa, preserving their ancient Coptic
Christianity as Islam swept across North Africa. At the beginning of the last century King Menelik II conquered vast stretches
of the savanna below, where the people speak languages of the
Oromo and Somali families and are Muslims or "animists."
Since the end of World War II, landlocked Ethiopia has been
trying to extend its territory to the Red Sea by annexing Eritrea.
Some fifty thousand people have died in the most recent phase
of the war, hundreds of thousands have been displaced. We
arrived during a cease-fire arranged by the Organization of
African Unity. It was summer; drought ravaged the lowlands.
The vast area called Ogaden that King Menelik II had seized,
now occupied by Somalian nomads, was in a continuing state
of insurrection against Addis Ababa. These things we knew
from reading the press in our own countries. In Addis Ababa we
learned nothing more from the couple of four-page newspapers

in English, published essentially for the foreign delegations from English-speaking African countries, and carefully censored. We met ex-soldiers returned from or deserted from the front; they had no idea where the front extended and if they told us why the war was launched they did so offhandedly, as if to indicate that that anyway was what they were told. They could speak of the government that took power upon the overthrow of Haile Selassie in 1974, the expropriation of feudal land-owners, the collectivization of the land, the civil war waged against it by the Tigrayans in the north, for Mengistu Haile Mariam had covered the country with billboards with slogans of the Marxism he had learned from the Albanians. But Mengistu was overthrown in 1991, and now the northerners are in power and Marxist directives have vanished, but nobody had an idea what, if any, policies the present government has for the country. We certainly were not making any sense of anything.

We met a middle-aged white man named Thomas married to a beautiful Amhara woman; his father had come here from Yugoslavia. During one long somnolent afternoon he explained in heavily accented and broken English his mechanic father's improbable life story in increasingly entangled detail. We only grasped that he somehow slipped between front lines during World War II in Yugoslavia and somehow ended up in Ethiopia, scene of an Allied invasion against Mussolini's occupation troops. In the yard out front there was a battered Land Cruiser, the 1967 model. We asked if we could rent it for a trip to the south. He agreed and told us he would supply an English-speaking driver and some tents.

That evening the driver looked for us at the hotel. He said his name was Belete, but as soon as he left we realized we had not committed it to memory. Balding, perhaps sixty, somewhat stout but sturdy, radiating a stabilized inner serenity, he spoke unceremoniously and offhandedly as though he had always known us. We liked him at once. He took us to a nearby night market where we bought provisions. We were skeptical of the piles of vegetables and dried meat and found instead packages of biscuits, tins of tuna, and some jars of chocolate sauce. He then told us that people we photographed will have to be paid, and took us to a black marketer where we got bundles of one-*bir* notes.

At six the next morning we picked up cartons of bottled water and set off. We were on the main highway across Ethiopia. The first hundred kilometers were being asphalted with, we saw, European Union heavy machinery and no doubt funds. Some forty kilometers out of Addis Ababa, Belete stopped the car on the bottom of a volcano and from the brim showed us the lake inside the crater on which the clouds of the sky rested untroubled. We watched the local women coming up from the lake with clay jugs of water. The first woman to notice us stopped, swung the jug from her head, and poured us clay cups of cool water.

At midday we stopped for lunch at a small dusty roadside place called the Bekele Mole Hotel. From then on whenever Belete found a roadside place to eat he judged suitable for fastidious foreigners, it was another Bekele Mole hotel. Out of some unconscious short-circuiting in our brains, we began addressing him as Bekele in the days that followed. We were taken aback and horribly embarrassed when, the last day of the trip, I found in my shirt pocket the name card that the Yugoslav had given us, with his real name Belete Gebre written on the back of it.

Soon we descended the Great Rift Valley, that gigantic crack in the continental plate that splits the mountain fortress of Ethiopia in two. At the bottom we were in the southern deserts. Bekele-Belete found us lodging at a Bekele Mole hotel, small rooms with mud brick walls. We were the only guests; this was a truck stop but the truckers on their way to and from Kenya slept in their trucks. Some of the trucks were loaded with bags of grain; these, Belete said, were being supplied by international aid for the famine-stricken deserts into which we were headed. Belete's English was simple but adequate, and in the days that followed we saw he also knew enough of the languages of the nomads to arrange things everywhere. At food stalls along the road he bought some of the dishwater-gray crêpes the Ethiopians call *injera* and some meat that he had the hotel woman cook for us. When we retired, a boy brought us buckets to urinate in during the night; the toilet was in back of the compound and dark.

It was the last of the Bekele Mole hotels, until our return back up this road. From now on we camped. Belete had found a stand of trees by a now parched and cracked riverbed the following night. No sooner had we set up our tents than we heard a crashing through the trees and four very large dark brown baboons circled us, looking indignant at our invasion. We gave them the supplies we had bought; they even seemed to like the chocolate sauce with tuna.

In the days that followed we drove through scrub desert where grasses were dead tussocks and bushes were leafless. From time to time we saw the skeletal remains of sheep and goats whose flesh had been consumed before they died of the drought. One day as we drove through a vast area that Belete identified as the Mago National Wildlife Reserve, we saw approaching us in a cloud of dust a Jeep and three stout men in safari khaki holding rifles; they did not hail us as they passed. "Hunters," Belete said. "Hunting is allowed?" Ken asked. Belete explained that foreigners pay the government big sums for permits—three thousand dollars for a kudu, five thousand for a lion, ten thousand for an elephant.

Belete's body, though not muscular, seemed possessed by the nerves and sinews of a warrior as he swung the Land Cruiser over potholes and ruts in the track, then found an unmarked fork to turn on and navigate down the desert. In fact he had a very precise itinerary in his mind; each day he drove us to a nomad market.

These were gatherings of a hundred, two, three hundred

people, where about a well there were stands of ragged trees. This, Belete would say, is the Tsemay market. This is the Turmi market. This is the market of the Bena and Ari peoples. We strolled about among the people as Belete found injera and someone to roast some skewers of goat meat for us. Markets, he called them, but nobody seemed to be buying or selling. There were not sheep, goats, or camels tethered for sale; there were not, as wherever else I had been in impoverished Third World lands, piles of missionary-supplied clothing being sold. There were no craft items that might have interested us to buy. Everyone was clad in the most extravagant garb of his or her own making, women in colorfully beaded goatskin skirts, their faces tattooed, their arms and legs ringed in embossed copper coils. The men had astonishing coiffures, their kinky hair close-cut with shaved lines shaping diagrams, imbued with white and red and blue clays and decorated with carefully placed feathers. Their skin was painted, very often their legs in white with arabesque designs. Usually it was a cloth band they wore about their loins, as though their virility needed no animal-hide emphasis. They each carried a small stool of polished black wood, which they rested on to keep the ground from smearing their body paintings and which also served, Belete told us, as a pillow sparing their headdresses when they lay down to sleep. The men, young and old, carried well-oiled and polished rifles and belts of gleaming bullets about their waists. Eventually we noted that there was something for sale in the market: some women were seated before piles of powdered pigments. And women were serving from great clay pots a kind of beer. We also saw that a man had brought an antelope he had been lucky enough to kill, but he was not selling it, he was celebrating: joyously distributing pieces to children and old women and to his friends who joined the feast with jugs of beer.

Feasts then were what these "markets" were. These people had come long distances on foot in the most spectacularly impractical garb. There were no officiants and no rituals scheduled for this day, no troop of entertainers, no singers or dancers to see. It was their own beauty they were celebrating. Indeed from halt to halt we began comparing their tall elegant stature, their perfect complexions, their noble features and radiant smiles. One day we gaped in astonishment at Karo people and decided that, men and women alike, they were the most beautiful of all.

For many years I traveled without a camera, thinking that it objectifies people with whom I wanted to interact, thinking too that there is something false and delusive in trying to fix and stock up images and situations from the past, thinking that it was the changes in my heart I brought back that were alone real. But one day a student friend took me to a camera shop where he was buying a new camera and gave me his old one. I left for India, and for days pointed the camera only at buildings and landscapes. Then one evening I was in a shikara, a gondola, on Dal Lake in Kashmir and I focused the camera on the willows that veiled the edge of the lake. As the boatman slowly rowed on I saw in the range finder that I had just snapped some men bathing in the lake. I looked up; they had seen me—and were shouting. They were grinning and shouting, "Thank you!" Pondering this, I realized that they were pleased that it was they and not the landscapes and monuments of India that I wanted to record. I was learning to take pictures by developing a roll at once—in any Indian town black-and-white film could be processed—and studying the results. I realized you can always find poor people again, they will be there the next day, or their acquaintances will be. And I soon realized that photographs of themselves, people who have no, and never will have, possessions, is the most innocent gift I could give them.

The people in the nomad feasts glanced away but did not turn their beauty from me. We would not come this way again, and these nomads have no addresses to which I could mail them their photographs. But I had become very greedy to take their beauty back with me. I ventured to take out my camera. It was impossible to be unnoticed; at once anyone I turned toward demanded one bir. I had arrived and turned the feast into a market.

In my country there are beautiful people who turn their pale emotionless faces and lissome bodies to cameras for millions. Here no doubt someone some years back had passed by, dazzled by the physical splendor and superb body decoration of the people, published his photographs, and then passed by again to show them to them. They had asked to keep the book, and were told it sells for fifty dollars. So they realized that if they were to be models they should be paid. One bir, I reflected, is U.S. twelve cents; the film roll works out to about that per frame. Any tourist who can afford twelve cents for a film frame can afford twelve cents for the model. On the other hand, for Ethiopians twelve cents is a great deal; wage earners in the capital get eight bir a day. The one bir I or other travelers pay them is the only source of money these nomads could have access to. I asked Belete what they do with the money. Buy bullets, he said, for the rifles they have traded camels for in Kenya.

Belete called us over; skewers of broiled meat were laid out on injera for us under a tree. The woman who had cooked them, a woman of about forty, was not especially attractive and her beaded goatskin skirt was worn. She had some tattoos on her weatherworn face, and but one piece of jewelry, a ring. Ken went over to her, asked to see her ring. One saw that it was a piece of thick aluminum wire coiled about her finger. "Trade?" he asked. She smiled shyly. Of course she did not understand the word. He gently removed it from her and replaced it with his.

II

The Old Hospital

I HAD SOMEHOW MANAGED TO GET A TICKET. Only
twenty-five were sold for each performance. Downtown
Rio de Janeiro, the control center where in high-rise buildings
the staffs of corporations and banks work by day, was now deserted. We waited inside the iron fence of the disaffected hospital that crouched between office buildings awaiting demolition.
But word passed among us that one section of the building
was still functioning: terminally ill homeless people the police
picked up from the streets at night were brought there to die.

Finally the doors opened. We stood in the dark entrance
hall; then on either side of us spotlights revealed, standing on
six-foot-high boxes, Yahweh and Lucifer, two old men wearing
robes of coarse cloth. Lucifer argued that Job was pious because Yahweh had showered him with all terrestrial blessings.
Suddenly Yahweh accepted the test Lucifer proposed. The
lights that illuminated them went off, and they vanished in
the darkness. We heard screams; then Job and his wife pushed
through us, she wailing over her children lifeless in her arms.
They staggered down the corridor. We followed. In niches
along the corridor stood robed figures chanting a dirge.

We arrived at a huge room, no doubt a former lecture or
demonstration hall; plaster lathes showed through patches of
the wall that has been damaged by rain. Two rats fled as we
approached, scrambling into the wall. Job's wife rushed back

and forth shouting, shaking her fist heavenward. Job sought
to calm her and silence her blasphemies. Two bare-chested men
descended upon Job, stripped him naked, then disappeared.
Job's wife climbed up on the balcony, raising her arms to the
darkness above, shouting out her misery and her defiance. She
descended, left the room, and staggered up a staircase. As we
turned to follow her, Job, now streaming with sweat and blood,
pushed through us. Most of us cast down our eyes before his
nakedness; a young woman swooned, was caught by others
before she fell. One of us, an old woman, reached to hold him,
her eyes red with pain.

Upstairs, we made our way along a corridor open on one
side; across the courtyard some of the windows showed dimly
lit rooms where we could see skulls and skeletons as used by
medical courses. We wondered which was the wing where there
were still beds with sick people. As we crossed over a catwalk
to the opposite wing, we contemplated a procession below us,
a priest dragging a cross followed by flagellants chanting a
Dies Irae.

We found ourselves in another large room, apparently a
former medical ward. Now there was but one metal bed stripped
of mattress pad. The ceiling had collapsed, showing the roof
rafters and tiles, and the rain had blackened the walls. Small
bats scudded through the dim light. Job collapsed on the bed.
One of his friends arrived and approached him and expressed
shock over his state. Then another, then a third. They were
clad in timeless coarse robes. Job's wife, shaking in anguish,
urged them to do something. At length Job stumbled out of
the bed, his body covered with scabs marked now by red lashes
from the bare springs of the bed.

He staggered out into the corridor; we followed him. The
corridor was very narrow and there were planks set on saw-
horses all its length so that we were pressed against the wall.
The first, then the second, then the third of Job's friends strode
across the planks. They recognized that they could not console

him as his afflictions continued unabated. They told him there must be some explanation for the disasters that had befallen him. Finally each raised the question whether he had not offended the Law, if only inadvertently or unknowingly. They elaborated their arguments, pacing up and down the length of the planks.

One after another they left. Job groped his way down the corridor. We found him in a small circular room. Most of the plaster had fallen from the ceiling and walls, leaving the bare lathes like bars of a cage. In the center there was a raised metal table. Over it was suspended a bright light bulb under a metal hood. This was the former surgery room of the hospital. We had to push together around the walls; the room was soon hot and the air dead. Job lay on the table, his naked body dripping sweat and blood on the metal of the table. After some time the door opened again and we recognized Yahweh, whom we had seen at the entrance at the beginning in the celestial dispute with Lucifer. Job turned on the table, then shifted off it and turned to question Yahweh. But Yahweh was now himself in rags, his aged body gray and covered with festering wounds. He stood there for some time, with nothing to say. Then he left; the door closed behind him.

Job hesitated only long enough to catch his breath, then shifted off the table and moved to the door. He opened it; the corridor outside was now opaque with luminous fog. One could see nothing through it. Slowly Job entered it. Into some kind of deliverance? Into madness? Nothing suggested an answer to our question. The light and fog slowly dissipated.

Finally we ourselves left through the dim and empty corridor, descended the stairs, crossed the now empty courtyard; looking up, we saw that all the windows were dark. But we knew that in one wing of the building lay destitute people, dying.

Outside the streets were deserted. In the office buildings that walled them there were floors illuminated where cleaning staff were working. I walked toward the bay and then down the broad park that borders it, occasionally hearing birds rustling in its luxuriant trees. Then I penetrated the long tunnel still full of the fumes of traffic that led to Copacabana. When the tunnel was bored, Copacabana became the most famous beach in the world. Only three blocks wide, walled on the right side by cliffs, Copacabana is the most congested urban area in the world. But now it is inhabited by lower-middle-class people crowded in its apartments; the rich and the elegant shops, clubs, and discos have moved to Ipanema and beyond. In fact it was rather safe to walk alone; the pickpockets and muggers would be gone during the hours when the tourists are asleep in their hotels. I walked in the street; on the sidewalks people, whole families, sprawled on flattened cardboard boxes were sleeping fitfully. Even in the heat of the night some of them clung to one another in sleep. Some of these people, I thought, have AIDS. I reached Avenida Atlântica; beyond, the beach sparkled under the moon before the black rumbling ocean.

III

Typhoons

CHARLES DARWIN DISCOVERED in the Galapagos flora and fauna that had evolved on those isolated Pacific islands; Madagascar is where biologists rush today. Not geologically a part of Africa, this "Great Red Island," the fourth largest island on the planet, is a fragment that drifted off when Pangaea broke into continents two hundred and fifty million years ago. Madagascar is known for its lemurs, protosimians found only there, but biologists have verified that virtually all the native plants, reptiles, and mammals on Madagascar are endemic species. Today the island's human population of fourteen million is projected to double within twenty-five years, and its rain forests—only 10 percent of which remain—are being slashed, burned, and logged. The oceans are red with millions of tons of soil being eroded from its mountains, its savannas, and its deserts. Hundreds of endemic species are on the brink of extinction.

When one thinks of going there—as a scientist frantic to catalog the vanishing species or a tourist curious to see lemurs or unique lizards and frogs—one learns that Madagascar is among the ten poorest countries on the planet. Its agroexport business collapsed when, after gaining political independence from France, its military rulers sought out Soviet economic and political advisers and expropriated foreign holdings without compensation. The socialist vision turned into an ideology.

Madagascar's current president, in power for twenty years, allegedly has millions in Swiss bank accounts while the country is bankrupt, under the tutelage now of the International Monetary Fund and the World Bank. Public funds go to maintain the bureaucracy and service the national debt; under World Bank–dictated public service cuts, three hundred schools have been closed. One will expect that any assistance from government agencies or police comes at a price. The traveler feels anxiety about his personal safety. He has little confidence in a personal or institutional ethics to hold back the impulses of mass desperation. The trip there has something of the feel of an act of recklessness and bravado.

A friend invited me to join him on a walk into the jungle. He had chosen the zone of mountains and swamp most inaccessible to loggers. We left Antananarivo in a taxi-brousse, descended to the coast, and went to the end of the road, then by dugout canoe to the beginning of the river. We trudged through muck, then up and down rocky mountains in the rain. It was exhilarating, but I lagged behind my friend, he so full of vigor and determination. We crossed a young Malagasy of about twenty on the path; he looked at me and with a smile and a sign offered to carry my backpack. I accepted. After a couple of days I wimped out. As my friend continued into the jungle alone, I lingered at a hamlet we had come upon, dried my clothes, got fed. The next morning, the young man who had carried my backpack appeared again; I indicated I was going back. He reached again for my backpack and set out.

He spoke not a word of French; I could not, by nodding my head and appealing to him, even learn the Malagasy words for "yes" and "no." He wore secondhand running shorts distributed by some missionary; my coarse cotton pants, purchased to protect my legs from leeches, rasped against my thighs and left them raw. He strode barefoot up the rocks and through the rivers; my jungle boots blistered my feet and filled with muck. He was always well ahead of me, or behind me; he would put down the backpack and wait a half hour to let me get ahead or would catch up with me. When the path forked I could only wait for him to arrive, or come back, to indicate which branch of the path to take.

In my backpack I had an expensive camera and six hundred dollars in cash. Were I he, sitting somewhere ahead or behind with that backpack, I surely would not resist the temptation to look in it. He could do whatever he wanted with my backpack, and with me, with impunity. I knew his name was Javalson, but where he lived I had no idea.

But when night fell he found a hut for us to sleep in and produced some bananas found or purchased somewhere. The next day we reached the river, and he found a dugout canoe to take me back down the river. Among the people gathered at the river's edge I found someone who spoke some French and asked him how much I should pay my guide and savior. Fifteen thousand francs, he pronounced, and indeed Javalson seemed pleased when I handed that to him: three U.S. dollars. He was gazing at my backpack: I opened it and wondered miserably what gift I could give him: I had given away all my medicines on the way and the inadequate food I had brought was gone. He pointed to my extra socks, took them with a grin; we shook hands, he disappeared. Of course, without shoes, he would not wear those socks in the muck and on the rocks; I understood he would keep them as a bemused—and affectionate?—memory of my absurd outfitting.

A few weeks later I was in London. In a spring sunshine that had not welcomed me there before, I explored its gracious streets, flabbergasted as one always is after a prolonged stay in destitute countries by the material abundance. That night, a Saturday, before going to bed I turned on the television and learned that a bomb had exploded in a crowded street in a London district inhabited mostly by blacks. A week later, again on early Saturday evening, a bomb exploded in a crowded street in a district inhabited mostly by Bangladeshis. The police determined that the bombs were simple explosives packed with nails that tore into and maimed people across the street, and that the bombs had been brought to these locations and left in a gym bag. The television did specials on skinhead and neo-Nazi gangs, showed Internet sites of hate groups, reported police investigations of linkages with American militia organizations and Serbian agents. Newspapers received letters claiming responsibility for the bombings from an organization called Commando 18 (cipher for Adolf Hitler). But the police revealed that they had infiltrated that organization and instead suspected a break-off sect that called themselves White Wolves. The television showed repeatedly a video from a street camera that had recorded a young man circling the area of the bomb the hour before it exploded. Hundreds of undercover police were assigned to Jewish and Muslim areas, awaiting the following Saturday. But on Friday early evening, a bomb exploded instead inside a gay pub in a crowded street in Soho. The three nail bombs had killed seven people and injured more than three hundred, some now in critical condition, others with amputated limbs and destroyed eyes.

Whenever I went out I found my eyes scanning the curtained windows of brick apartment blocks, behind which people conduct their business shut from prying eyes. As evening fell it was not in the empty side streets but in the crowded streets that I began to feel the pervasive fear.

Two days later the police, tipped off by neighbors who had recognized the young man in the video, raided an apartment and found bombs made with materials that could be purchased in any hardware store, and packed with nails. They arrested the tenant, a young engineer of twenty-three, and the next day reported they were confident that he had acted alone.

For three weeks the media had run specials by criminologists, sociologists, and culture critics analyzing the skinhead, hooligan, and neo-Nazi subcultures in democratic and prosperous Britain, specials on immigrants and racism, on the culture of violence on television and in pop, punk, and rap music. Civic leaders, beginning with the prime minister, called for a national examination of conscience on the pervasive and unremarked racism of everyday life and attitudes and for a national commitment to the rule of law and to multiculturalism. Now the newspapers and television channels ran specials on the genetic, biochemical, and social causes of criminal psychopathology.

For days the image of this young engineer hovered in my brain, and the image also of that other young man on the trail in the Madagascar jungle.

A history of foreign invasion, colonial oppression, economic exploitation, then a violent struggle for independence followed by homebred dictatorship and bankruptcy reduced an island twice the size of the British Isles to increasing illiteracy and desperate poverty. Add to that the trauma of forced imposition of foreign culture, religion, and language, the local society corrupted, its religion discredited. And yet a rich foreign visitor, there to take a vacation trek in the jungle, finds he is secure alongside a local man encountered by chance on the path.

The motherland of modern democracy, a Britain confident in the new European community, prosperous, with five centuries of the rule of law behind it, a people identified for the value of fair play, a city priding itself in its cosmopolitanism and multiculturalism—there a young engineer, acting alone, makes the whole population, including this American visitor, afraid to walk the streets on a Saturday evening.

To be sure, social scientists, psychologists, and ethnobiologists elaborate explanations: in an overpopulated and ecologically devastated place like Madagascar, excluded from the multinational corporate global economy, where the imposed modern national and political systems work only for the profit

of a military oligarchy, the destitute young man subsisting
in the jungle returns to his ancestral tribal culture and cults,
which place preeminent emphasis on mutual aid. In the high-
performance, information-highway, retraining and recycling
economy and culture of contemporary Britain, a young engineer who does not fit in, victim of some childhood or adolescent trauma, has no cultural backwater to retreat to and finds
his only effective force is his indiscriminate hate.

All that can and must be said, if we are to understand. But
as I listened to the political scientists, sociologists, cultural critics, religious leaders, psychologists, and ethnobiologists explain
on television, I found myself going back to the very experience
of trust, and of terror, that I had known. In that experience
there glowed some inner understanding that I had to bring out.

Knowledge induces belief, belief in what one sees clearly or in
a coherent and consistent account that supplies evidence or
proof. Trust, which is as compelling as belief, is not produced
by knowledge. In trust one adheres to something one sees only
partially or unclearly or understands only vaguely or ambigu-
ously. One attaches to someone whose words or whose movements one does not understand, whose reasons or motives one
does not see.

Is it all the things that are known that encourage the leap,
in this one instance, to adhere to something unknown as
though it were known? Is it not because of a long past tried
and true that someone becomes a trusted adviser? Is it all that
one knows about the laws, the institutions, the policing, and
all that one knows about the values, the education, the peer
pressure of individuals in a society that induce one to trust
this individual met at random on a jungle path? But the more
one knows about a tried and true adviser, the more clearly
one sees that every act of loyalty opened an opportunity for
disloyalty. The more one understands about the laws and
programming of a culture, the more clearly one understands

how they are imposed upon, but do not eliminate, can even provoke, impulses contrary to them.

Trust is a break, a cut made in the extending map of certainties and probabilities. The force that breaks with the cohesion of doubts and deliberations is an upsurge, a birth, a commencement. It has its own momentum, and builds on itself. How one feels this force! Before these strangers in whom one's suspicious and anxious mind elaborates so many scheming motivations, abruptly one fixes on this one, at random, and one feels trust, like a river released from a lock, swelling one's mind and launching one on the way.

I determined, at a glance at this young man whose words I could not understand, to trust him to guide me out of the jungle. To have put trust in him is to have to put still further trust in him, each time he was a half hour ahead or a half hour behind me with my bag. Once trust takes hold, it compounds itself.

The one who finds himself trusted knows the path because he has trekked it regularly, come by this way just yesterday, but he knows that in this rain mountain paths collapse, rivers crossed yesterday may be untraversable today. He knows there is much he does not know; he trusts himself to be able to deal with the unknown when it shows itself. He then counts on his trust of himself more than on his knowledge. Once one puts one's trust in him, this trust can only generate yet more trust. The force of the trust one puts in him makes his trust in himself the dominant force in him, dissipating his anxieties and vacillations.

Trust binds one ever more deeply to another; it is an energy that becomes ever stronger and more intoxicated. Upon watching Javalson leaving me at the edge of the river, how I felt I had known him so much more deeply than if I had listened to someone who had, the length of an evening, recounted his life to me in a language I could understand!

The act of trust is a leap into the unknown. It is not an

effect of ideological, cultural, historical, social, economic, or ethnobiological determinisms. But trust is everywhere—in the pacts and contracts, in institutions, in forms of discourse taken to be revealing or veridical, in the empirical sciences and in mathematical systems. Everywhere a human turns in the web of human activities, he touches upon solicitations to trust. The most electronically guarded, insured individual is constantly asked to trust.

"He was a good neighbor, didn't bother anybody, always polite," the neighbors said of the London bomber—neighbors say each time a monster is identified in their midst. Someone you trusted to rent that spare room to, you trusted to keep an eye on the baby while you went down a few blocks to get some groceries, turns out to have been making bombs to kill innocent strangers indiscriminately. Trust turns into terror. A cause, an ideology, a group marginalized in the dominant society, or a vendetta does not explain the solitary bomber. He was not a member of the White Wolves. Because the police suspected he was, because they saw racism in the first bomb in the black neighborhood and the second in the Bangladeshi, they did not foresee that the third would explode in a gay pub. Like trust, does not hate too arise beyond or even outside of knowledge, outside of reasons to hate, and feed on itself?

The psychologists and criminologists look for reasons for a hate that first flared in the infancy or adolescence of the young bomber. Was he abandoned or abused as a child? Traumatized as a pubescent adolescent? But we have to recognize that hatred is not the direct reaction to someone or something detestable. The young engineer, who still hated his father who had sought to socialize him, could have despised him instead or now consign him to insignificance. He who loathed his father who had sexually molested him could have instead used his father's libido as the excuse to liberate himself from parental authority and affirm his own virility. If hatred arises, it goes beyond reasons to despise or condemn. Before the father's order, hatred pushes aside the inclination to explain and justify oneself, to acquiesce or evade. Hatred is a force that breaks loose. It has its own momentum. It seeks out reasons or excuses to hate on. When the father is just chatting amicably with his friends or just dozing on the sofa, hatred feels the more free to intensify its force and indulge its virulence.

That is why the one whom one hates, even if he is one's father or she one's ex-lover, becomes someone generic and anonymous. I hate my spouse for her castrating words, but at the moment she is visibly someone just making our evening meal; to sustain my hatred is to dissolve this image of someone who enjoys cooking. Before hatred, she becomes more and more "a bitch," "*the* bitch." For this young engineer, those before whom his hatred first arose had inexorably become "the others." Thus it could seem to him that his hatred acted effectively in wiping out strangers in a black neighborhood. Once he heard the indignant television reports lament that the dead and injured were random strangers, his hatred could find in random strangers in any London district its target.

Opposition can be measured and counteracted, but hatred is feared. Fear is fear of what is unknown; it is not simply a reaction to the manifestly dangerous. Before a mountain path one knows will give way if one steps on it one either refuses to advance on it or else feels a resigned acceptance of death; it is before the mountain path whose stability is unsure that one feels fear. It is not the Commando 18 agent known and identified by the police who spread fear across all London's neighborhoods but someone possibly acting alone and without ideology who might explode a bomb anywhere, or who might stop his activities and live somewhere in London without those three bombs ever being attributed to him. Because the unknown is without mappable boundaries, there is also an inner spiral in fear, which suspects in the unknown yet ever further circles of the unknown.

The one who hates feels the force of his hatred in the waves of fear that spread about it. And those who become ever more fearful and irresolute intensify the hatred of the bomber, whose hatred extends to ever more indeterminate others.

Fear in turn flows into, becomes, hatred. The hatred of the solitary bomber ignites the hatred of millions against him and also against any polite young engineer who keeps to himself. Were it not for the fact that only the laboratory staff studying videos from the street cameras and the desk staff in the police stations studying their files could identify and locate the bomber, and that the police officers arrived by stealth in the neighborhood and sped him away in an armed vehicle, he would have been lynched by his neighbors. The specials the television featured with psychologists and criminal pathologists were not only broadcast in order to satisfy the public craving for understanding; they were also broadcast in an effort to smother the flames of public hatred. Human rights organizations warned the public against antiterrorism legislation that would curtail their own liberties. They fear that the police equipped with forensic and detective science and rigorously controlled by parliamentary legislation are themselves instruments of terror. The citizens come to fear, and thus to hate, their own terror.

The individual one does not know and entrusts one's life to and the solitary individual one can only be terrified by each exist, then, in a social, economic, historical, ideological, cultural system that does not completely produce or explain them. Trust and fear-hatred, like typhoons launched by the fluttering of a butterfly, emerge and intensify with their own momentum. Since they seem to be opposites, the mind would like to think that they exist in a dialectic. Educators are sure that only acts of trust can put out the rage in delinquent children; parole officers extend measured trust to convicts whose bitterness has smoldered for years in jails. They are right to do so, for trust is as strong as fear and hatred.

Yet in the rice-terracing economies of Cambodia and

Indonesia, economies that for hundreds of generations required the most intense social cooperation and evolved the most self-less ethics, the most barbaric and senseless massacres break out. In the center of prosperous, cosmopolitan London, a solitary bomber strikes.

São Paulo

O N A SIDE STREET in downtown São Paulo there is a woman of about thirty, not unattractive, seated on some flattened cardboard boxes against a doorway. She has a baby, a large doll. You see her when you go out of your hotel; she is there when you go out in the morning, in the evening, when you come back in the night. She never looks at you or holds open a hand to you. A few times you have seen her wash in the fountain in the adjacent square. You have noticed the waiter from a cafeteria at the corner bring her a plate of food after mealtimes. She does not cling to the doll, rock it and coo over it as a little girl does; often it is left to her side as she contemplates the passing scene. Like a real baby it often seems to tire her or bore her. It is always warm in São Paulo; a fixed awning overhead shelters her from the rain. She has a pile of extra clothes. She never begs. She is not a little girl. There is nothing she needs that she does not have. There is nothing she wants. Except someone, something to love. Haggard, unrelenting, craving to give.

You eat, sometimes, in the adjacent cafeteria. The waiter is young, vigorous, his face has a certain charm. He is certainly ill paid. He surely does not live around here; he must take a long bus ride here each morning from one of the far-flung favelas that extend the city. In your country he would be a student or apprenticed to a trade. After the meal hour he takes her a plate of food, handing it to her, not looking at her, not speaking to her. He understands it is not the craving to be loved that is in her.

She must have learned as an infant. She must have learned, playing with a stray puppy, that her frail body is full of pleasures to give. Holding that puppy, but not too tight, her baby hand learned tenderness. In contact with the puppy mouthing and licking her legs and fingers and face she learned that her hands, her lips are organs that give, give the pleasures of being kissed. Trusted to watch a baby sister while her mother went off to work all day, she must have learned that her hands, her thighs, her belly are organs that give pleasure. In a slum childhood, abandoned to the streets, she learned how little she needed or wanted. Picked up, fucked, left by a fifteen-year-old, and by how many men since, she learned how little she needed or wanted. How much all that tenderness, all that pleasure she learned she has to give aches in her now!

One day she was gone. You blamed the police. This is the center of the city; was there some business conference for foreign investors in town, so that the police were ordered to clean up the streets, clear out the riffraff? Was there some national commemoration to be made—some historical event to be celebrated, some statue to be unveiled?

But a few days later, you saw her again. Seated at the same doorway. With the same doll.

One day you left São Paulo. You saw her as you left the hotel with your bags. She is still there. You still see her. She, who did not need you or want you, got born in you. You who had no need of or desire for her found her to care about and care for. You who after all have so much tenderness and tact, kisses and caresses, to squander.

A Man

THEIR FATHER IS NOW INFIRM AND INCONTINENT, she told me—and egotistic, demanding, and cantankerous. He had been fit as a bull, and then had this stroke. They were unable to afford the costs of a nursing home. Their father had treated her tolerably as she was growing up and she could reason with him, but she lives in a two-room flat and holds down a job as a copy editor in a publishing house. Their whole childhood, she remembered, their father never stopped picking on her younger brother, beating him up, ridiculing him. Her brother went on to marry a waitress who works at a truck stop. He works nights on a city road construction gang and still goes dancing on Saturdays. Once their father could no longer take care of himself, her brother without discussion arranged for him to be moved in. She herself has had enough of the bilious and querulous behavior of their father and, when she visits, has to leave within an hour. She can hardly believe that her brother takes no account of it. But her brother is visibly not asserting any kind of dominance, not taking his revenge.

She was silent for some moments. Then she said she realized her kid brother had grown up and had become a man. She said that was all there was to understand. And, if questioned about it, all that her brother would have to say.

The distinctive male traits—penis and penetrator in copulation, greater size (20 percent, on average) than females, and different pattern of and, usually, greater muscularity than females—materialize distinctively male sexual and social behaviors. They co-determined the original division of labor in societies. Male identity and pride can issue in practices of dominance and brutality.

Masculinity is seated in "secondary" differentiating characteristics of the male body—the angularity of the male body, the specific hirsuteness, the deeper tonality of the voice. Masculinity denotes appearance and also demeanor and behavior and is elaborated in distinctive speech, gestures, postures, and garb, and in courtship, teasing, and games, the domain of seduction.

We are indeed impressed by someone superlatively male. One prizes one's own consummate maleness. Who is not awed by the splendor of a bull, a buck antelope, a ram, a male silverback gorilla? And—noblesse oblige—one expects such males to be enterprising and forceful in actions. We are captivated by the glamorous masculinity of medieval knights and samurai, nineteenth-century cavalry and naval officers, bandidos decked out in black and silver, and high-society con men, suave and charming. Knights, bullfighters, and skydivers compound male splendor with masculine glamour.

But what we especially care about is being a man, a real man.[1] Virility is what we look for not in our foreman, manager, commander, or protector, but in our buddy, our companion.

Virility is not simply an ethical trait, produced by character management and determination. It requires the chance of a body that is sexually excitable, that has the physical power to be courageous, the strength to impose justice.

The virility of a bus driver, a window washer, or a junior executive asserts itself in sexual arousal before a woman who denudes herself before him deliberately and provocatively or a naked woman caught sight of by looking down upon a bedroom

or shower room window. It is aroused before a male deliberately
flaunting his nakedness or unknowingly being watched. When
he is no longer compulsively aroused by a chance body contact
in the subway, a chance view into an apartment window in the
next building, a man recognizes the loss of his virility.

A virile adventure is one in which one finds oneself seduced.
The perhaps otherwise integrally servile individual—the soldier, the factory worker, the computer programmer—who feels
the surge of virility before a naked body feels the provocation
of hope, the pull of despair and terror.

The surge of virility is the feeling of nakedness in oneself, the
nakedness of one's glands, one's penis, the compacted coursing
of blood and passion. It is the compulsion to throw off one's
clothing, one's uniforms, one's categories, one's responsibilities,
to give oneself over passionately to a destiny marked out by
chance events and apparitions.

One who knows the surge of virility in himself is attached
to it but not as to a goal or an achievement. He laughs at his
erections, his obsessed nights. His laughter recognizes that his
manliness does not point him to what the corporals or corporations recognize as an objective, nor to what his own intentions and ambitions recognize as good for himself, nor even
what would be good for the denuded stranger he has caught
sight of. One who plays with chance runs risks, in ignorance
of the game being played by others. His laughter assents to all
bad as well as good luck; his laughter celebrates license and
puerile pleasure, innocence and wickedness, festivity and op-
portunities lost.

The physical radiance that one did not create, nor did one's
parents, destines one for what lies beyond usefulness and service-
ability. How often we have seen in the brightness of a factory
worker in Oklahoma, the flair of a dockworker in Haiti, or the
dash of a rickshaw puller in Pakistan physical splendor so extra-
neous, so irrelevant to these jobs and this subordination!

What chagrin to see someone recognizing his beauty, flair,

style, and setting out to use them! We do not see virility in the fashion model or personal trainer whose body is the product he sells or rents.

In making oneself useful, in character planning, in getting trained, reprogramming one's movements, one's forces, one's circadian rhythms with functional diagrams for useful operations, one subordinates one's body, mind, and will to the layout, equipment, and operation of a factory, an office, a corporation. One keeps at bay nature where roses bloom without why and the rain falls on the nettles as on the wheat; one lets oneself be banished from the sovereign world of the stars, the winds, the volcanoes. An assembly-line worker, a supervisor, a security guard, an electrician, a computer programmer, a junior executive are divested of virility. The perception that the modern corporate workplace has no place for virility—nor for womanhood—is expressed in today's zero-tolerance policies for any kind of sexual images or words, policies readily adopted by giant multinational corporations. Maleness may well serve the lean-and-mean corporation; virility defines outlaws.

The office worker goes off, for the time the company allows him once a year, to the wilderness to find his virility. He goes not with fellow workers, whose varied competencies reconstitute a team in the wilderness camp, but with his adolescent son, in order to find again the incompetencies and risks of his own adolescence.

To give oneself over to the omens and coincidences that signal the path of a destiny implies a specific strength of the body. Fitness and expertise insert the body into a productive system; the courageous body is a body attuned to chance, to hope and terror. Virility requires courage.

The simple deployment of massive male size and musculature without adventure and risk brutalizes others but also brutalizes oneself. The self-indulgent intellectual, whose skin not exposed to the sun is pale and dry, who has the sagging stomach of men who indulge in nocturnal cogitation inscribing words over their visceral sensations—to invoke courage in such a one is ridiculous. Courage is not involved in the professionalized shaping of the body in training and discipline. It is absent from commercial body culture, that exalted in celebrities and advertising, and from the fitness that a junior executive maintains as part of his image.

The highest strength is not the mobilization of the musculature of the body by an industrial, military, or athletic program. Courage is the trance into which a body is cast by the chance vision of a great hope and great risk. "It was the head tracker's marvelous swift response that captured my admiration at first," John Hersey wrote, "his split second solicitousness when he heard a cry of pain, his finding in mid-air, as it were, the only way to save the injured boy. But there was more to it than that. His action, which could not have been mulled over in his mind, showed a deep instinctive love of life, a compassion, an optimism."[2]

We see another's courage by feeling the pounding of that very courage in us. Our trust then is not an assured dependency on his courage but a surge of courage in ourselves. For trust requires courage.

The courage that mobilizes the body is shadowed by its simulacrum, muscular power entranced not by chance but by certainty—by a political or religious doctrine that gives itself out as truth. In the measure that, in the determination of storm troopers pledged to an ideology, certainty drives out chance, brutality replaces courage.

Virility is lost by giving up. By arranging for alibis. And by selling out.

One sees them everywhere—ill-groomed, self-indulgent suburbanites seated before televised football games; on city sidewalks gray-skinned, gray-eyed men in business suits whose bodies one cannot imagine in any other garb. By the age of forty they have given up; they still have half their lives to live but have decided they will never be seductive to other humans.

Giving up begins by giving in; it begins in comfort. It begins each time comfort enters as a factor in any decision. It begins when one does not go down the Grand Canyon because the trail is hot and dusty and the mule the guide is offering you lurches, when one does not even go to Italy and France because of the hassles of not understanding the language and not digesting the food, when one did not set out to escape czarist Russia by hiding in a hay wagon by night.

For how many men the press of family and professional responsibilities, economic necessities, the importance of a long-term job function as alibis! Alibis for not being set on fire by chance nakedness, alibis for not ecstatically opening one's eyes to the fierce bird of hope and risk soaring in the skies of chance. He took on this summer job in case a buddy would roar by on a wreck of a motorcycle and shout, "Let's travel the hemisphere!" He hastily married and sired a child in case his buddies would rush off to join the insurrection. How many family and professional responsibilities were first taken on in order to function one day as an alibi for not taking chances, not plunging into passion, not fighting for justice!

One loses one's manhood by selling out. One exchanges the hot passions of youth—passions for eroticism, ecstasy, and justice—for the cold passions of age for wealth, power, and fame. How much cowardice is there in the greed for wealth, power, and fame! Indeed everything one despises in oneself turns out to be some cowardice.

Manliness—that is to not take anybody's shit. It is also not to shit on others, and not to let anybody shit on others.[3]

Injustice—the use of one's strength and brightness, flair, and dash to acquire the goods of which the needy and the talented are thereby deprived—makes one lose one's virility in greed, self-indulgence, and brutalization. Nature does not distribute its goods according to need or merit. Virility, the force at grips with chance, strives against the injustice of bad luck. Virility is maintained in the passion for justice.

Virility gives force to anger. Not the violence unleashed in frustration, that is, in weakness, nor the bluster of unoccupied and peevish brutality, anger is the force of inner vigilance against comfort, alibis, and corruption. Anger marks out what is unjust, inadmissible, intolerable. It casts itself from the first beyond the perception of what can reasonably be expected or demanded. It exercises a refusal, a resistance, an intractable vigilance.

You were nicknamed by your comrades "el Gallo"—the rooster, the cock. Once while at dinner at your grandmother's house, you went into the kitchen and, with the door open, suddenly turned and embraced the maid and made love with her. Your friends saw how lusty you were, but you were always guarded about sexual encounters, even in your diaries. They were never "conquests." Your first steady was beautiful and intelligent but rich. You came to dinners at her family mansion in the un- washed shirt you had worn playing rugby all week. You mar- ried a Peruvian half-breed when you learned she was pregnant. When your child was born, you left for combat. During the years of the insurrection, to protect women who had come to fight from being sexually used, you enforced separate quarters for them. One night one of those women could not sleep and went out for a walk. You were driving by in a Jeep, and stopped. "What are you doing here?" "I couldn't sleep." "I am going to attack Cabaiguán," you said; "do you want to come?" "Sure," she said and climbed into the Jeep. "And from then on," she recalled years later with a playful smile, "I never again left him or let him out of my sight." You married her and four years later left her for combat again. The only trust fund you would leave them would be a world in which a little more injustice would be fought against. On another continent a woman turned up, unable to forget you from a chance meeting in Eastern Europe, and stayed with you in the struggle against all odds, the struggle that was to end in disaster.

Long into maturity you had that adolescent body. You had those fiery black eyes, voracious and malicious, under high arched eyebrows. Your forehead was sculptured with over-hanging brow, your nose was fine and sensitive, your lips full and supple, exposed under the thin arc of a mustache. Your curly reddish beard sprouted late into adulthood. Women spoke of the beauty of your intense gaze, your smile so tran-quil that it overturned one's heart. They spoke of your quick movements, your sprinting gestures, though your body was not high-strung but calm.

Barely surviving pneumonia in childhood, you fell victim to asthma so severe you had to be taken to a resort town in the mountains. You were too sick to go to school; your mother tutored you. You excelled in rugby. You climbed the highest mountains in Peru and in Mexico. You would sleep only a few hours. The strongest men saw your adolescent-looking body choking with asthma outlasting them in endurance. All your life the asthma attacks threw you into the panicky convulsions of a drowning man.

But it was not your own state of bad health but the weeks you cared for your dying grandmother that motivated you to change from engineering studies to medicine. You were a doctor who never had an office and not once wrote a bill for services rendered. Wherever you happened upon someone afflicted by a harsh blow of chance, you stopped to clean and disinfect and bandage. After every battle your first priority was to bind the wounds of your fallen enemies. You befriended despised animals, stray dogs, and mules, you kept a white rat with you and played with it between raids and battles.

You were already reading Rimbaud and Freud at the age of thirteen. Your phenomenal intelligence rose out of experi-ence in combat, in social administration, in diplomacy, in a diversity of cultures. In the Andes, in Algeria, in Egypt, in Ghana, in India, and in Japan your flashing spirit spotted the most curious things and greedily feasted on them. You wrote that you would serve the new state for five years. You held a key administrative post, but fed your family on the common rations. Your associates told of a long meeting about urgent matters that lasted the heat of the day: you never opened the thermos of coffee someone had set beside you. When asked why, you muttered, "There wasn't enough for all." You spent the weekends working fourteen hours a day without pay on the docks or in the cane fields. Those who were working alongside you stole glances at you from time to time, seeing in your unselfconscious brightness and unadorned style a blessing that chance cast in their lives of deprivation and desperation.

You were in exile from earliest manhood. You quickly relinquished the position of authority to go to other continents to offer your forces and your life wherever men and women suffered oppression. You said that every real man must feel on his own cheek a blow that strikes the cheek of anyone. You once said to a woman who asked about your family because she thought she might be related to you that if she felt indignation over injustice anywhere on the planet, she was your sister.

You have been, in the last half of the twentieth century, the single most admired man in all the lands whose injustice you marked out with your anger. Your image will continue to be found on the walls of huts in the slums of Latin America, Africa, and Europe, and we will continue, from time to time, to put in words some of the things you mean to us.

October 9, 1967, La Higuera, Bolivia. 1:10 p.m. The sub-officer Mario Terán has volunteered to carry out the order to shoot the prisoner. But when he is about to enter the building, he is trembling with fear. The prisoner is seated on the floor, shoulders against the wall. His leg wound has stopped bleeding. He sees his executioner trembling, and says, "Shoot, coward, you are only going to kill a man." Terán steps back, shuts his eyes, and fires. Then with eyes shut he fires again wildly. Another soldier comes in to fire finally the shot that puts an end to the life of the prisoner.

"Che"—originally a Guarani word equivalent to "buddy" or "mate," alive in Argentinean popular usage after the Guarani Indians had been exterminated. Also used as "Hey!" "Wow!" "Can't be!"

Our Che, our buddy, our comrade.

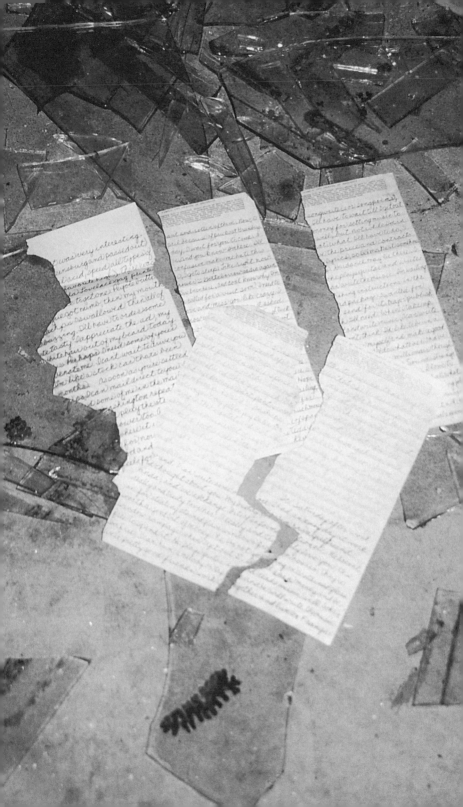

Letters

THIS HAPPENED A LONG TIME AGO. I think about twenty-five years ago. A lifetime ago. It was a late November day, overcast and cold. I was coming from out West with a younger friend, driving toward Pittsburgh. I began to talk about Pittsburgh, a city where I had taught for six years, and began to remember where I had lived, in a little house next to a huge wooded ravine behind the bluff called Mount Washington overlooking the city. The house had two rooms, an attic loft, and a basement for the furnace, the toilet, and the kitchen. I had rented it for thirty-five dollars a month. The house was left over from a miners' town that had been perched over the ravine. I had pulled up the linoleum and sanded the floors, glued burlap on the walls, built a worktable, opened the old fireplace, planted spring bulbs in the tiny yard. Describing my old house awakened in me a desire to see it again and show it to my friend. We detoured into the city. When we arrived at the house it was vacant. We walked around to the back and found the door bashed in. We saw that the neighborhood kids had broken the windows, bashed at the walls, even torn up the stairs and floorboards. We stepped across floor rafters and piles of fallen plaster, I telling my friend what the rooms looked like when I lived there, filled with melancholy at the realization that this was the last time I would see this house; now in ruins, it would be torn down under orders of the city. My friend noticed some torn papers and began collecting them: they were letters torn once through the page, top to bottom. I took some pages to the window and tried to read them in the fading light. My friend kept searching for more pages in the debris, but he kept bringing me only the right or the left half of a torn page. Many pages must have been blown out of the broken windows into the ravine below. I read sentence fragments out loud at the window as it got darker and colder. They were letters to a woman from a young man in prison. He recounted his news—for even in the utterly routinized days of a prison there are occasional events: new inmates, fights. He also spoke of preparing for the time when he would be released: he was cutting down on cigarettes every day, doing more and more push-ups in the cell, writing songs he would play when he had a guitar again. But mostly he wrote of her, invoking every part and organ of her body, recalling in graphic detail the things they did with one another's bodies in the woods, in the creek, in the truck, in an elevator, next to her mother's bedroom, recalling with pleasure all the pleasures he had been able to give her.

I was getting more and more troubled reading these letter fragments. We were eavesdropping on a torrid love. In the cold and dark, in the ruins of my house, reading these torn pages, I was overcome by a foreboding that this ended tragically. How could she have torn up these letters? Once in your life you receive a letter, a succession of letters like that. Most people never receive letters of passion. Most people never know what it is to be loved like that. With what conviction he wrote, his incarcerated body so overfull of that good thing, all that pleasure of love he had to give! She must have worried about these letters, not known what to do with them. She had taken everything out of the house when she left. I imagined her taking the mattress, the chairs, armfuls of dresses, bags of kitchen utensils into the pickup truck. The letters she had taken out of some box, put them aside on the mantel. Now she had everything, and it was time to go. She turned to the letters on the mantel, burning like acid. Abruptly, with violence, she snatched them up, torn them once down the middle, dropped them, and fled the house. I was sure that that was what happened.

It was now quite dark in the house. My friend brought me two more half pages; these matched two of the pages I had laid out on the windowsill. He had written: *Red came to see me on Saturday and brought me news of you, and why you had stopped coming or writing to me.* With firm hand he had written: *No one will ever love you as I love you.*

Song of Innocence

*O*NE NIGHT OUT OF SO MANY a man and a woman embraced in love and you Nancy Gilvonio were conceived.
Who was conceived might not have been you. You might have
slipped from the womb stillborn. You, *charapa*, half Indian,
were born alive near the town of Tarapoto on the Amazonian
side of the Peruvian Andes.

The cement and the board buildings of Tarapoto, the
parched laterite roads, the cleared fields, and the trees beyond
exist because they have existed. To see them is to see their past,
full of them. When now you look at your past, you find your
childhood, your infancy, your birth. And before that, nothing
of you. How light is your birth, not laden with the weight of
a past it has to answer for! In the past of this ancient land, its
emergence from the primal oceans, its inhabitation by peoples
come long ago in the Ice Age from remote regions of Asia, its
incorporation into the Inca empire, its conquest by Pizarro
and his thugs, yesterday the coming of lumber companies and
explorers for petroleum, there was nothing whatever of you.

"My child," your mother says. She cannot help seeing in
you her body that composed and nourished your body. As you
begin to coordinate limbs and senses and pick up patterns of
doing things in the house and in the town, she and your father
cannot help seeing "our" in you—our child. But you are not
them. It is not in your physical traits and sense of what you

are—a girl, a charapa—but in your existence that you are a stranger to them.

A child, you are not on your own. Your mother and father are there to keep you alive and growing. You leave the burden of carrying on the projects initiated in the past and the task of securing resources for the future to them. You play out your existence. One day you can take on responsibility for the past they are carrying forward. But your birth, the innocence and newness of existence in you, is repudiation of the past and irresponsibility.

To be born is to awaken to the world. Each morning you Nancy Gilvonio awaken and are flooded with light. The dark of the night with its confused intrigues and sorceries has passed away without leaving a trace. Joy awakens, joy is awakening. You wake up to the amorous murmur of the forest. You wake up to the huge eyes of a grazing alpaca, enigmatic as a song brooding over a love lost centuries ago. Years later you awaken in a night truck lurching around bends in the mountain road to Lima. You wake up in the cold misty silence of an abandoned peasant hut in the high mountains. Joy gives you Nancy Gilvonio the strength to open your eyes to all that is there without being foreseeable or understood. Your awakening is innocent and just even if it changes nothing in the course of the world. Even if it subsides, even if it fails.

Your father and your two older brothers labored a plot of the cleared and so quickly leached-out ground to grow food. Your mother chopped at the earth to plant and then later to dig up roots and tubers. Your childish limbs began to coordinate; you washed and dressed your younger brothers and sister, prepared food for them during the day when your mother was away. Each year you took on more and more tasks about the house, then in school. You worked hard at your lessons and began dreaming of going on to higher education. And one day, against all odds, you Nancy Gilvonio set off to San Marcos University. With but one change of clothes in your bag you climbed on a truck and three days later you arrived in Lima. You made sociology your major. You worked as a cleaning woman in the upper-class neighborhoods of San Isidro to pay your rent and books. You are short in stature, lean, with a narrow face and very broad and deep eyes. Your black hair is straight and long. Your skin is pale brown flushed with clay red as though always lit by a twilight sun.

The work your father, your brothers, and your mother did was not really participating in the immemorial rhythms of peasant life. They interrupted field work to take up whatever labor jobs turned up, some legal with road construction and logging gangs, some smuggling of merchandise and coca. The field work, the meals, and the laundry your mother went to collect in the town and scrubbed at the well have the nature of tasks that come to an end. Even if they have to be begun again in the morning after the discontinuity of the night as though they had never been done, they have to be begun again because they had been finished the day before.

The interruption of continuity makes possible the leap, with all the forces of the present, into what is ahead. It makes possible hope. Hope is hope by rejecting the evidence of the past, by being against all odds.

One day in a forgotten corner of the czarist empire my father, who had never been to school at all, son of a peasant who was the son of a peasant who was the son of a peasant, to escape the czarist army draft burrowed into a hay wagon and crossed the border into East Prussia, there to confront and deal with whatever confronted him. One day in the town of Tarapoto on the Amazonian side of the Peruvian Andes, you Nancy Gilvonio climbed into a truck with strangers. Two innocents, two children.

You Américo Gilvonio walked through the town of Tarapoto and worked its fields with the woozy sense of how much your voice, your musculature, your body hair, your genitals have become manly by contrast with your brother Raúl two years younger than you. You vividly felt how much your know-how, your thinking had changed each year; you found it awkward that there was always a gap between what you thought and what those two years or even a year younger than you thought. There are immense solitary trees in the forest that are not cut down, that shelter and guide you when you walk through the forest. You Américo Gilvonio listened to the voices of such trees, for they know how much there is under the earth and in the heavens; they know the matter the stars, all types of roots and waters, insects, birds, and worms are made of, and this knowledge they, embracing you with their shadows, extend to you. One day you watched the columns of minuscule ants, who have made a home for themselves in the sweet dead core of a tree, streaming over the leaves of that tree to clean it of fungi and diseases, glittering like red stars in those dark green leaves.

The flowering plants about the home are wilting in the sun. The weeds are choking the rows of beans. A child you come upon is crying from hunger or cold. The dog has a thorn in his paw. The immense solitary tree requires you to stop and hear the music, wisdom, counsel, and immortality it whispers. Your future lies there before you, a circumscribed field of work awaiting you in Tarapoto.

You Américo Gilvonio, charapa, half Indian, are growing strong in waking up to what you have to do. One day you came upon a jaguar, free, sprawled over the limb of a tree contemplating you, contemplating some wild and lordly animal in you. You know that what you have to do may require fierce and unyielding hatred.

After the Great Rebellion of 1536 and the final conquest of Qosqo by Pizarro, Manco Inca retreated to a stronghold in the inaccessible fastness of Vilcapampa. Four Incas held together their people there until, in 1572, the Inca Tupac Amaru was lured out for battle and then hunted down in the Amazon jungle. He was given written assurances by King Felipe II of Spain that if he surrendered he would be treated as a prisoner of war. Tupac Amaru surrendered to save the lives of his people and was dragged by the conquistador horses to Qosqo. In the cathedral square, under the eyes of the viceroy Francisco de Toledo, the bishop, and the priests of the Inquisition, his wife was mangled in front of him. His head was struck off and stuck in a pole set up before the cathedral standing triumphantly on the foundations of the residence of founder Inca Wirakocha.

Before the spectacle of the superstitions and errors, greeds and despairs, cynicisms and brutalities, complicities and betrayals that is the history of our species, philosophies of history claim to track a pattern, plan, or meaning. Then historical events and processes become understandable or explainable. Looking back, what looks like crisis, violence, and chaos has to be assigned instrumental significance. This historical understanding would not be accessible to individuals whose field of action is staked out by their own urgent needs. But a ruler who acts to shape the course of his times has a philosophy of history.

In far-off Lima funds were arriving from the World Bank and from Japan, arms from Argentina and Israel, military advisers from the United States. President Alberto Fujimori abruptly shut down Parliament, imposed a state of emergency, and launched an all-out military campaign to exterminate the armed opposition, the Sendero Luminoso and the Tupac Amaru Revolutionary Movement.

An army unit arrives in Tarapoto. People are stopped, interrogated, disappeared. Behind closed doors at night, women share their anxieties; in the fields men speak with men from other towns, men who have spoken with truck drivers from faraway towns. For you Américo the horizons abruptly widen and you see the field of work awaiting you in Tarapoto inserted into the broad expanse of the lives of the charapas, cholos, zambos, Quechuas, and Aymaras of Peru. You know someone in the next village who has contacts with the Tupac Amaru Revolutionary Movement. You

abruptly determine to join the armed rebellion. You confide
in Raúl, who passionately declares he will go with you. You
will fight, with all your strength, for a renewed birth of your
people by the arms of your united comrades. What fiery joy
this will awaken in you!

Four days after the atomic bomb incinerated Hiroshima,
small plants began to take root in the ashes and began to make
ground for themselves with their own fallen leaves.

In 1988 you Nancy Gilvonio learned that soldiers had arrived one day at the hut in the muddy clearing near Tarapoto;
they were looking for Américo and Raúl. They repeatedly beat
your father, pouring water to waken him each time he sank
into unconsciousness. They left him crippled. You Nancy left
your studies in the university and returned to Tarapoto in
a truck to try to earn money so that your parents and sister
would survive.

You Nancy Gilvonio one day awake in a shanty near the
town of Tarapoto in the Amazonian rain forest that extends
below the icy mists of the Andes. You watch the clouds swivel-
ing in the blue, the leaves of the trees braiding the wind, listen
to the birds chattering in the downpouring night. Years later,
to awaken in this shanty is to be born innocent and irrespon-
sible, the alien world kept at a distance.

One breaks with the continuities, one takes action. Action
leaves effects and also leaves traces of itself on you, a diagram
that can be varied, can be stabilized as a skill and a habit. And
does not a successful action fill one with pleasure or at least
with satisfaction? But your deed and its glory are on their own
now, and you find yourself the next day with empty hands
once more. Action of itself produces a discontinuity, a return
to emptiness, to innocence.

You Américo hardly had to learn how to exist and operate
in clandestinity; as soon as you leave Tarapoto your name and
your family name have left you, your body and your non-
descript clothing are those of anyone about you. Who will ever

tell how or why you were seized? Your torturers tell you that
your brother Raúl has cooperated with them and that if you
cooperate you can see your brother. Has Raúl already been
disappeared? you wonder in anguish. You lie on the floor of
this cell, waiting for them to return, to torture you once more
or this time to bludgeon you to death. You are alive only in
this waiting, these hours of waiting. They take you once again
and you look up at the empty sky, vast and hopeful as the
future. You hold tight to your silence as they bludgeon your
body in some army barracks until it is a nameless corpse to be
thrown in a pit outside under the raging sky.

The sky overhead unites all who breathe under its seamless
space, uniting us to all who are born and shall be born under the
sky—you and me and Nancy and Américo and Raúl Gilvonio.

In the anonymous body of a fugitive, astonishment greets
improbable beauty. In the inexplicable splendor of a woman's
courage, of a man's heart, love welcomes the unknowable. In
the force of the passion for justice, love quickens.

One night a man covered in filth sought out the shanty
in Tarapoto where he woke you Nancy Gilvonio who lay in
an exhausted sleep always threatened by terror. He had come
to tell you what he knew of your brothers, his comrades. He
tells you he grew up in Balconcillo. You knew that working-
class slum in Lima. During a strike at a textile factory he had
been arrested. In prison his closest friend Hermigidio Huerta
had had his eyes gouged out with a rifle butt and had then
been beaten to death by the police. This man had escaped the
prison and fled Lima into clandestinity, where he had known
Américo and Raúl. His name was Néstor Cerpa Cartolini.

When he left the next night to make his way to the Tupac
Amaru hideout, you Nancy Gilvonio went with him. Always
clandestinely, always moving, always ever more in love, your
life was raids on army posts on the roads and flights into the
mountains the Indians knew. How fierce is your love! That
year, 1988, a son was born to you, and a second was born five

years later. You Nancy cannot help but think of your dead brothers when you gaze upon them.

What is this great power that makes us able to make love to this person this night as though we had never made love to anyone before, to make love to this person this night as though there will never be anyone again?

On November 30, 1995, Nancy Gilvonio was arrested. She was identified to the press as a terrorist but she had been beaten so badly she was never shown. Nancy Gilvonio did not reveal anything of Néstor Cerpa Cartolini, not his whereabouts, not his activities; she denied knowing anyone of that name. One day she was shoved before a hooded judge who sentenced her to life imprisonment in the Cárcel de Yanamayo, a redoubt on top of a thirteen-thousand-foot mountain in southern Peru. Her unheated cell is six by ten feet with a narrow slit in the wall that lets in icy winds but no beam of sunlight. Her bed is a cement slab, the latrine a hole in the floor. She is locked in there for twenty-three and a half hours a day. She is allowed to receive a visitor for fifteen minutes once every two months. She is allowed no reading matter or exercise. If Nancy Gilvonio is still alive, she is there as we wait with our words.

How much succeeds that is made of greeds, deceits, and betrayals! What succeeds finally comes to be deemed beneficial. About the one who failed, if his action left no beneficial consequences, it left no consequences. One says that he was wrong to think he was justified in acting as he did. But in the space his action left innocent of consequences, the passion for justice that flared in it is still seen.

In death, every life fails. It disconnects from the processes of history. If it is true that its enterprises may go on by themselves, one no longer pilots them, and they are taken over or brought to a halt by others who live. In letting go of the controls, in disconnecting, in dying, there is innocence. That is why the corpses of criminals too are treated with respect.

Nancy Gilvonio, half-breed, improbably born somewhere on the Amazonian side of the Peruvian Andes, entombed, disappeared. *Nancy Gilvonio, mistress of Néstor Cerpa Cartolini, alias camarada Huerta, alias camarada Evaristo, alias El Gordo. Terrorist of the Tupac Amaru Revolutionary Movement,* which military and civilian counterterrorism experts judge is now down to not more than thirty to forty members still at large.

Combat is the art of the possible. When there are resources and forces one can count on, their effective use depends on exact knowledge of the forces and movements of the enemy, the elaboration of an ingenious strategy the enemy could not have foreseen, and the resolve to maintain the most rigorous discipline. Bravado is what one invents in impossible situations.

With the capture of Tupac Amaru in 1572, the conquest was complete. With the beheading of Tupac Amaru before the cathedral of Qosqo, the conquest was ensured, extending for the subsequent four hundred years to our day. 1996: in Lima, Alberto Fujimori speaks on nationwide television. The forces of order have prevailed. The population of the capital have seen the last of power blackouts and car bombings. The president announces an ambitious plan to attract foreign investment and set up institutions to train workers in technological skills. Security, order, and peace have been established in all Peru.

People everywhere manage their lives and their interactions with one another, answering situations with ordinary decency. Chimpanzees get along with chimpanzees, deer get along with deer, penguins with penguins, dolphins with dolphins, wasps with wasps. Even predatory and solitary animals get along with their own species: leopards do not prey on other leopards, eagles do not hunt down eagles. Can we spend our lives ensured that no extraordinary demand was put on us?

At 8:14 p.m. on December 17, 1996, at the elegant garden party honoring Emperor Akihito's birthday at the Japanese ambassador's residence in Lima, more than six hundred guests were sipping whiskey, nibbling on sushi, exchanging *abrazos.*

But an ambulance had just unloaded a handful of people into a house next door. A moment later, an explosion silenced the festivities. Through the dynamited wall of the adjacent building, masked guerrillas burst upon the garden party. At once a firefight erupted between the police in and in front of the compound and the invaders. Holding off the police, the guerrillas herded the six hundred guests inside the embassy and sealed it.

How many were these guerrillas who had taken six hundred hostages, without anyone being killed or even injured? The press counted between twelve and twenty. They were men and also women. The hostages included thirty-five Japanese businessmen, six military and police generals, the chiefs of the intelligence and the antiterrorism bureaus, seven foreign ambassadors, six national congressmen, five Supreme Court justices, two government ministers, and President Fujimori's mother, sister, and younger brother. Japanese businessmen included senior executives of Mitsubishi, Mitsui, Toyota, and Panasonic. The top power structure of the oligarchy and the police of this police state had been seized in a feat unprecedented in the history of guerrilla war.

At eleven o'clock that evening 280 women and older people, including Fujimori's mother and sister, were released. In the days that followed all but 72 hostages were released.

The guerrilla commando issued its unique demand: that the 442 Tupac Amaru prisoners, including 89 women, be released in exchange for the freedom of the 72 hostages. The commando was led by Camarada Hermigidio Huerta. Hermigidio Huerta is the nom de guerre of Néstor Cerpa Cartolini, Nancy Gilvonio's husband.

Prime Minister Hashimoto of Japan flew to meet with President Fujimori in Canada, to pledge him not to endanger the lives of the hostages. Each day the Red Cross delivered food to the hostages, including meals from Lima's best Japanese restaurants for the Japanese inside. The Cardinal Archbishop of Ayacucho, the Canadian ambassador—who had been one

of those in the Japanese ambassador's reception but had been
released the first night—and a representative of Fujimori's government were instructed to negotiate with the Tupac Amaru
guerrillas. But Fujimori only offered safe conduct out of the
country to the terrorists if they released all their hostages
unharmed.

Fujimori gave secret orders that a SWAT commando be
constituted and trained by the U.S. Special Forces, and that
miners be recruited to tunnel from a distance toward and
under the grounds of the Japanese ambassador's residence.
At the state prisons journalists and also the Red Cross were
denied access to the 442 Tupac Amaru prisoners.

Four months passed. To break the nerves of the guerrillas
the police broadcast military marches at top volume toward the
residence. Negotiations were intermittently broken off. The
guerrillas released two more hostages who had developed
health complaints. One was General Luis Valencia Hirano,
commander of the state antiterrorist police, who had developed
a stomach ulcer.

Lives that have been shattered and irreparably broken
sometimes show singularly little bitterness and instead defiant
composure, uncomplaining and undaunted and finally laughing. Their affliction and their bravado have made them deep
but also childlike, innocent, insolent, and impetuous. In many
cases it is necessary to hope for nothing in order to undertake
any action.

In March, the guerrillas detected, through the blare of
the military marches, the faint rumble of tunneling under the
residence. They moved the hostages to the second floor of the
building. After four months, it was clear that the negotiators
had instructions to concede nothing. Inside the residence, the
guerrillas felt the future and the past fallen from them with all
their weight, leaving these last moments disconnected, buoy-
ant, and with all their energies held and intensified on these
moments. They spent their afternoons playing soccer.

On April 22, in midafternoon, while the guerrillas were playing soccer, multiple explosives opened the tunnels, and the government SWAT team broke through. The troops shot dead all the guerrillas, including two unarmed women. They were found to be fourteen. In the pandemonium one of the hostages, a Supreme Court judge, died of a heart attack. The thirty soldiers of the SWAT team circled around the bodies of the slain guerrillas, each one firing shots into the head of each corpse. After President Fujimori, in front of the press cameras, stepped triumphantly over the mutilated bodies, they were taken to the army base and then buried in an unrevealed and unmarked grave.

A letter was found, written the day before by Néstor Cerpa Cartolini to his nine-year-old son, whom French sympathizers had been able to spirit out of Peru to France. The letter read: *If I ever leave this Japanese residence it will be because I have achieved what you are waiting for and dreaming of: having your mummy out of prison, being able again to see her, touch her, play with her and be in her arms.*

Addis Ababa

*I*N HIS STRONGHOLD on the highest mountains of Africa Emperor Haile Selassie, Lion of Judah, 237th in the dynastic line that claimed descent from Menelik I, son of Solomon and the Queen of Sheba, had grandiose visions for his capital. Addis Ababa was to be the headquarters of the Organization of African Unity, of the countries that had emerged from centuries of European enslavement and colonial subjugation. He laid out new avenues and studded them with proud new buildings for the various institutions of the OAU. He invited Hilton and Sheraton to build five-star hotels for the diplomats and their staffs. The population of Addis Ababa, now swollen to two million as a result of decades of war with Eritrea and Somalia, civil war, drought, and famine, continues to expand the shantytowns that from a respectful distance surround these great buildings.

I had to go to the bank to get funds transferred to me. The National Bank building is one of the most impressive in the city center, designed by a French architect. A great circular building set high on a pedestal, it occupies its own block and is surrounded by a high iron grill fence.

As I approached the bank, there was a woman with her two young children seated on the sidewalk under the midday sun. One child sat a few feet from her, not looking at anything. The woman listlessly held the other child against her with one hand. The children were clad in filthy rags. The woman's torn dress had fallen from her shoulders, exposing her shriveled breasts hanging from her skeletal chest. There were dark blotches on her skin. Though there were a few coins on the sidewalk about her, she did not hold out her hand to me to beg as I approached. Yet she was there with her children, for her children.

Nobody knows how many people in Ethiopia are infected with AIDS. A doctor I had met said perhaps 15 percent of Addis Ababa. Only the very rich of the ruling elite can afford imported retroviral drugs. In the hospital for the destitute where he works, they do not even treat the opportunistic infections that attack the patients. But people do come there to die, on hospital cots rather than in the streets.

When I emerged from the bank I hesitated long on the front steps of the building. Finally I went down and, with my heart pounding like that of a torturer, slipped between two parked cars and pulled out my camera, and from a distance and with shaking hands snapped a photo. I looked up; the bank guard had seen me, but he did not reproach me. I walked on and then from a distance looked back: he went up to the woman and ordered her to leave.

The next day I walked by the bank building again. The woman and her children had disappeared.

What else could it be, to recognize another person, if not to listen? To listen to a story, someone's story. For each one of us to recognize our own existence in the midst of buildings, sun, rain, mud, strangers is to tell our story, if only to ourselves. When, back in my country, I had the film roll developed at a shop in a giant shopping mall, there was only the thin bent smear of black on the silent paper of the photographic print. Yet I looked at the print and saw her and her children too as though she were there in front of me, in the aisle of the mall. I see her blinded by the midday Ethiopian sun, not seeing me, her wasted hand supporting her child in the last extremities of love. In writing this I know I am returning to her, though she is dead by now. This inability to depart from her, this desperate weakness, is perhaps also love.

Love Junkies

I HATE LIES, I would not tolerate lies from anybody. I've
always been like that, you Wayne explain.

What passion finds is the child and the child in the old man,
is the man in the woman and the woman in the man, is the
leopard, serpent, mollusk in the man or woman and the man
and woman in the bull, swan, crocodile, and octopus.

Billions of tons of salt water coursing around the vast Pacific
brush against the south coast of New South Wales, detaching
bits of rock and sod, spreading layers of sand sparkling below
the town of Cronulla south of Sydney. Sand of vast coral cities
built by multicolored polyps, demolished by ocean storms, sand
that tufts of salt grass hold on to, that are swept back into the
ocean by storms.

You Cheryl were born and abandoned in Cronulla. Somewhere a woman had met a man, they disrobed and embraced
and parted, and silently you started to grow in that woman.
The woman bore her pregnancy and then put you somewhere,
and disappeared. You have no idea why you were not wanted.

A Swiss couple adopted you. They called you Paul. You have
a brother whom you never see. He cannot understand your sex.
Your foster parents always called you Paul, until a year ago—
when, during what was to be their last visit, for they have moved
to Queensland and are very old now, you made them call you
Cheryl. They do, however, approve of Wayne. They love him.

You Wayne were born in Belmain, a working-class district of Sydney. You have a brother too but were separated from him when your parents divorced and your mother took him, your father took you. One day your father sent you to the shops to buy a newspaper, and when you came back there was five cents missing in the change. He flogged you with a feather duster for almost an hour and a half, trying to get you to admit that you had spent those five cents on lollies. But you hadn't and you wouldn't say you did to get him to stop. You hate lies. Your father started dating another woman and you were in the way. He charged you with being uncontrollable and put you in a boys' home. You were seven years old.

Junk velvets the hard edges of things. It's a silver fog rolling over all the cubicles, partitions, walls, and fences. How long is it that you have been shooting up, Wayne—thirty years? You Cheryl—thirty years in silver fog? There is plenty of junk around now, but you are on methadone. Wayne too. The maximum dose. You claim it is for the pain. It makes you spacey and hyper. You especially Cheryl are always fidgety and skittish. Medical researchers are now saying that methadone is more damaging to the organism than heroin. The idea is to progressively reduce the dosage. You Wayne and Cheryl are still on the max.

Your soul Cheryl is twitches and quiverings in the algae curtains of the stomach, the somber blue intestines, in the liver, the spleen, on the tips of your fingers under lacquered green fingernails. Your soul Wayne is turbulence and bluster and crystal calm in the blue veins, the slow heavy vermilion blood, the scurrying macrophages, the dense jelly of cells stirring the murmurs from years ago and far away.

You Cheryl are five foot nine, big-boned, very skinny, skeletal; right off you say your age: fifty-two. Your face is long, you have high cheekbones, your cheeks are sunken, your lips medium thin, your mouth small, delicate. You have very big brown eyes. You have shaved your eyebrows and you pencil in lines first thing when you get up. Your hair is thick and fine, brunette turning to blonde, cut short, combed to one side. Your very big hands are somewhat discolored with bleached pink, your fingernails clean and a little long. You have a gold watch with a very big face, a man's watch, loose on your wrist. You dress in moss green jail T-shirt and shorts, much faded, much patched, and on your feet, worn running shoes. About your neck you have a long string of small shells, the kind Filipino kids try to sell on the beaches. You keep two mirrors on the table; as you work you check your face, touch it up. You are a queen, if in green shorts. For nudibranchs creeping over the sands at the bottom of the surf, for naked frogs in the Sydney slums, for moths circling lights on the prison walls, beauty is imperative.

There is something giddy in our relationship with a mirror. Spaced away from ourselves, our gestures turn into grimaces, our manipulations into flailings, and our face screwed up by our scrutinizing gaze breaks into laughter. Looking at oneself while laughing releases lascivious impulses in our mouth, tongue, fingers, loins.

When you look in the mirror, you Wayne say, you either see your best friend or your worst enemy. You are a little shorter than Cheryl and maybe seven years younger. You have broad shoulders, strong arms, flat stomach. Your skin is very tanned. When you were outside, you several times ran the marathon. There are only migraines, nausea, insomnia in that body now. If your body does not shrivel and sink into itself, it is only because you are pumped with steroids. You are wearing a loose moss green long-sleeved light sweatshirt, light sweatpants— also much faded, much patched—and new good-quality runners. Your head is round, you have a thick black-brown walrus mustache, your mouth is small, your lips sensual. Your mouth is not sunken, though they have pulled out all your teeth. You have clear blue eyes. You look English, with your smooth pasty pale skin, your full head of bristly gray hair cut short in back.

You are well groomed, very particular about your appearance. You wear two small silver rings in your left ear. You wear a silver chain with a Masonic cross. On your left hand you wear four rings, one on your right. You Wayne are handsome. Handsome and impish. You have a dry sense of humor. And a hellish hot glint in those clear blue eyes.

You are not at all sly. People know you would do anything for a friend. Just ask you. There is nothing you Wayne can't fix. You have earned twenty-eight certificates for computer courses. You type résumés for staff people; screws bring you their computers from home to fix some programming glitch. You are a sensitive bloke. You are very civilized. You are always very pleasant to the female staff. You are respectful of women, and respectful of Cheryl. Cheryl devotes herself to you, to entertaining you. You treat Cheryl very well.

Males, with their on average greater musculature and on average 20 percent greater size than females, do hard work in agriculture, industry, and construction. They tear up streets with air hammers, they weld oil derricks in the Timor Sea, they paint the bridge over Sydney Harbor, they man peacekeeping forces in East Timor, they are professional boxers. They are expected to maintain order and system. They are at least expected to do contracted work, even if something trivial or pointless has to be found, to pay their own expenses. Lazy chiseling parasitical louts are an affront to their own maleness. But nothing so fevers the mind as a man swanking his gamy good looks.

In fact you Wayne adore Cheryl. You say that if she dies you will die with her. You will certainly kill yourself to die with Cheryl.

The voluptuous embrace is necrophilic, bodies collapsing, decomposing, already soaking the sheets and themselves with body fluids releasing spasms, musks, microorganisms. The flames of pleasure ignite them in clothing, in swampy stains on the wood of the furniture, in the air whose minute spheres of water vapor teem with protozoa, in the soil decomposing into unnameable fungi and bacteria.

You Wayne play computer games a lot. Your moves zap electronic people, detonate cars and planes, pulverize whole populations. You're a fighter. You have been in and out of institutions since the age of fifteen, your existence the piece of bad luck that society found in itself. You never had goals to give you a sense of yourself. Your sense of your individuality comes from being isolated from society in institutions. Throughout your street-kid childhood you were not, like the rest of us, continually told what not to do and why not. They didn't tell you why not. One can just see how you would react if some bloke came along and said, "Let's rob the bank." "Okay, let's go," you would say.

You robbed, but it was petty shit. It was not to change things, to break out and become somebody; it was only to keep up your habit. Again and again you were caught and sentenced. This is your twenty-third year in prison. Eventually they win, they get it their way. Now you are in the middle of a fourteen-year sentence for armed robbery. Long Bay gaol is a maximum security prison; you are in the company of everything society gets in the way of real shit luck: switchblade stalkers, gangsters, child molesters. Murderers radiant with the blood they have shed stalk the prison with lewd authority.

Among them you met Cheryl, twenty-two years ago. She'd been in for dealing, stealing. Factory women have rough hands and dismissive eyes, career women have manipulative fingers and skeptical eyes that repel the cloying eyes of lust. What else did you Cheryl have to do but be beautiful? Prostitution was the only source of wages you ever figured out. You Cheryl and Wayne became lovers ten years ago.

It's you Wayne and Cheryl we engage in talk with when we visit the jail, or want to hear about from those who do. You are delinquents and deviants, and not just victims of society that we have to feel guilty about. Your story is going to be funny—funny peculiar and funny ha-ha.

There are no end of things that one cannot prevent, ward off, overcome, or repair. One got born looking like a dork. One had an abused childhood. One got oedipally triangulated. One discovered one had a queer gene. One got caught up in a relationship that was hopelessly fucked up. There are so many things that one can do nothing about. Could do nothing about them at the time, can do nothing about them now. So many things that all one can do with is laugh. But one can always laugh. One can laugh at one's having been born with a ruin't gene, looking like Olive Oyl or Newt Gingrich, at one's micro-dick, about death itself. A neurotic is someone who is trauma-tized, that is, cannot get over these disasters. Cannot laugh. Psychotherapists are hardly any help. How tight-assed they are, by and large! They take everything the neurotic dreams over, broods over, so seriously. Every put-down from earliest child-hood, every humiliation. They seal the neurotic in his neurosis.

You've had a lot of fights in your time Wayne, though you've never been stabbed. You got iron-barred once. The bloke that did that lived to regret it. You'll cop a lot of shit before you'll explode, but when you explode, you really explode. The first time is accidental, you say; the second time is coincidental; the third time is enemy action. You'll cop shit on yourself; you won't cop shit for Cheryl. If someone upsets Cheryl, then that's it; there's no second chances. No chances at all. There's people in this jail that don't necessarily like you; they got to respect you for the fact that you'll live and die for Cheryl. The truth is you have more friends than anybody.

There are long scars on your arms Wayne from fights, but most self-inflicted. Your hands and arms are covered with tat-toos. On the base of the fingers of your left hand the letters L O V E. A tattoo you made, using a sewing needle stuck on the end of a toothbrush handle and activated by a motor you took out of a Walkman—you are very good at things mechanical!—keeps on your right arm your love for Diane Darling who had been a star performer at a transvestite cabaret on King's Cross and who died of AIDS in jail. You don't consider yourself a poofter, nobody else takes you for a poofter; they think: it's jail sex. Cheryl though fifty-two calls herself a girl, calls herself a queen. She has small plump breasts. She had, long ago, her testicles removed. You Wayne adore Cheryl. And in this, in your adoration of Cheryl, you are getting your own way in something at last!

Feeling the warm thigh of the somnolent passenger next to us on the bus, the hot breath of an excited woman bidding at an auction, the caress of a young monk in a Tibetan monastery amused by the down on our Caucasian arms, we are aroused. The penis stiffening, the labia and clitoris throbbing with blood and excitement and pleasure are the parts of our bodies that never lie.

On your right arm Wayne you have a large cross, with *In Memory.* Your uncle was a biker, finally crashed and smashed both his knees. When he died you were not allowed to go to the funeral. In jail doing a tattoo on someone is cited as bodily assault, doing a tattoo on oneself as self-mutilation. You did this tattoo and then went to the warden and told him to cite you. This uncle had taken you when at the age of eleven you got out of the Boys' Home and put you to work in his carnival. You worked the cars, roller coasters, Ferris wheels. You traveled with the carnival all over Australia. Carnivals have a bad reputation: people think there'll be fights and they have to lock up their daughters. You do have to use force: when a couple of blokes come up for a ride, they are not inclined to put down their cigarettes and beer bottles. So you got into fights.

Hate can be cold, ingenious, devious. Love is lawless, volatile, and violent. The adoration that breaks out of us violates our integrity and breaks up our individuality. To be smitten by love is to be not simply wounded, but shattered. Your adoration Wayne is the inner experience of being violated in sexual embraces and of violating Cheryl. Your love Cheryl is a craving to be violated.

The ocean fog has settled in the stones of Long Bay gaol a hundred years ago. The foul breath of caged men has settled in those stones. The toilets are ceramic bowls without partitions to separate the stink of one man's shit from another's. You Cheryl are fanatically housebound. You have amazing energy. You are high on washing and folding your and Wayne's laundry. Laundry is always happening.

You get up very early. You like to be maternal. You busy yourself darning socks, mending and altering the clothes of the men, skinny mother of brutes. You make small alterations that eliminate a bristly discomfort in a garment, that make the most threadbare garment fit and even flatter its wearer. You are ingenious. You vacuum all the floors of the education department. You take the vacuum to the apartment and vacuum it till there is not a wisp of dust lodged in any corner. You call the cell the apartment. It is only six feet wide, ten feet long. There is a bed bolted to the wall, a toilet, a sink, a jug, a Walkman. The cells are all open to the corridor, with only iron bar gates.

Many people really dislike you. The staff, but also inmates. You are sneaky. You steal stuff people are using. You are a two-faced bitch. We have to be careful about what we say around you; you will blab about it. You trade in gossip. Whether we are a new inmate or just a visitor, you will have heard all about us before we get there.

To be incarcerated is to have no life outside. There is nothing to an inmate but his inner life. To be on top of all the gossip is the way to touch, probe, grip on to the inner lives of others, who have only inner lives. Gossip is the only way one has in jail to have an intense inner life, penetrating and sizzling with pleasure. Gossip is a pleasure. Pleasure of pursuing prey, of intervening in melodramas, intellectual pleasure of ingenuity and cunning.

The consummate feminine look is that blasé look, that vaporous look, that impudent look, that cold look, that look of looking inward, that dominating look, that voluptuous look, that wicked look, that sick look, that catlike look, infantilism, nonchalance, and malice compounded.

You Wayne insist that Cheryl be treated with respect, and you are violent enough to insist. Because Cheryl still has her penis, she can be housed in the men's section, and with you Wayne. The authorities like homosexual couples forming—it reduces the general aggression in the jail.

Harmoniously married couples outside spend at least eight hours a day apart, at their jobs. You Wayne and Cheryl are locked in a six-by-ten-foot cell together all but five hours a day. When you are working at your jobs you are also together. Because Cheryl's a woman in a men's maximum security jail, it's not safe for her wandering around by herself. If you hear a scream you know where the scream's coming from, you know where to go. Sometimes you Wayne are with Cheryl twenty-three hours one day; the other hour you are in some office working on a computer—and strange as it seems to people, you miss her for that hour! I hate it, you say. I hate it.

Why is it that it is the jeering or derisive remark about our sexual identity, appearance, behaviors, or words that smarts most? Why do we so easily turn being called peculiar into being distinctive, being called eccentric into being exceptional, but when abnormal means abnormal in our sex it is demeaning and mortifying? How transparent we are to one another in our lusts!

You Cheryl became a woman when you were fifteen. You trained to be a registered nurse. You were caught stealing drugs and dismissed. You drifted to King's Cross, where part of joining the scene was drugs. You did heroin, speed, cocaine, bennies, acid. You're not into pot. You performed as a female impersonator in the cabarets of King's Cross—Les Girls, Simone, Candy. Back then you had toured the jails. Carlotta now acts in the weekly show on TV called *Beauty and the Beast*. She still writes you twice a year, sends you the programs of shows.

The numbers drag queens do depend entirely on surprise, their effects momentary. Surprising the aggressor with a put-down so witty he finds himself unable not to laugh at himself. The master in oriental martial arts is one who catches the lunge of the adversary and throws him with the force of his own blow. Zen and the Art of Drag.

You Wayne and Cheryl are the top of the heap. You are very sharp on people. You see what is going on. You can make things happen. You do the clerical work for the education program. You earn twenty-four dollars a week. Money is clout; the ordinary prisoner can earn but eleven or thirteen dollars a week. You get real coffee or chocolate biscuits, sometimes, from the staff. You get conversation about the outside world. You even contribute to decisions—for example, about how the money is spent in the education program. Just now you Cheryl are in charge of some repairs and painting that are being done in the wing. You love organizing people. You would have been a very successful businesswoman. You and Wayne are chummy with the superintendent. You can put in a good word for a bloke if his parole is coming up.

You Wayne and Cheryl believe that a real relationship—not just a relationship like yours but even a relationship between two good friends—can't last if there's not total honesty at all times. It's something you never got from your families, so it's something you've always demanded from your friends and the people around you. In my time, you Wayne say, I've probably met ten to fifteen thousand people in jail these many years that I've been here. Out of those there's probably a hundred that would say that I'm their friend; out of that hundred, there's probably sixty that I would call my friends; out of that sixty, twenty that I would say that I know they're honest and up-front with me and I trust them implicitly, and out of that twenty there's five that I would die for or kill for.

A bloke name of Xavier had made his way from Brazil to Australia as a mule for some drug smugglers. They caught

him. He was very mechanical. Out of bits of wire, discarded
tin cans he would pick up, he made clocks. Big clocks, covered
with glitter, with photos of cheesecake women, mug shots of
criminals, car crashes from magazines. His whole cell, all the
walls, were eventually covered with extravagant, hallucinat-
ing clocks. He was terrified of being transferred. One day,
they did transfer him to another prison. The following day he
was found murdered. He had not done his time. At the main
entrance of Long Bay gaol, there is a small shop where visitors
can buy artifacts made by the prisoners. The prices are fixed
by the prison staff. The most popular items are aboriginal dot
paintings; galleries in Sydney fix very high prices for aboriginal dot paintings, and they are much sought after in the world
art market. After Xavier's death, the shop put on an exhibition
of his clocks.

You Wayne and Cheryl have used your clout with the staff
to get in disinfectants strong enough to kill the HIV virus, for
use with needles. There is heroin enough for all in the prison,
supplied of course by the screws for those eleven or thirteen
dollars the inmates can earn. You Wayne and Cheryl have also
insisted that a condom dispenser get installed, but they then
mounted it on the wall next to the officers' quarters. So blokes
have to expose their intentions to the screws, and expose themselves to their shouts and jeers.

How foolish two people get when they become lovers—
how infantile their speech, how naive their sentiments, how
frivolous their behavior! How awkward, how ridiculous are the
gropings and thrashings of people copulating, how empty the
aimless repetitions of caresses, how mindless the compulsive
buildup toward orgasm! We lock the door, pull the drapes.
In sex theaters, all the movements are choreographed to be
graceful and synchronized; nothing is left to the directness
of lustful urges. When in the force of momentary grabbings
and repulsions they do show through, we are repelled and
embarrassed: suddenly we see what we do in our lovemaking.

We free ourselves from our embarrassment by giggling, and outside the theater guffawing over what we saw.

But when we spy on others and cannot help laughing, this laughter spreads through our body and reverberates in dissolute and wanton impulses. Telling and hearing dirty jokes do not make us superior and aloof from lustful urges; they make us sink into our sensual nature. In laughter we are transparent to one another, the peals of laughter not expressions of an I or of a you, spreading like waves about a pebble dropped into a lake, with no more individuality than waves.

The lust that disconnects the body from its tasks and its seriousness and releases it on the languorous and agitated body of another is nothing but the laughter of that body. The throbs, the convulsive repetitions, the upheaval, the absurd pleasure of the bodies in lascivious excitement are the laughter not apart from, but in those bodies. They have locked the door and pulled the drapes so that their laughter may be uninhibited, one and undivided. Orgasm is the vortex of the generalized laughter of bodies.

The working-from-within-the-system seventies, the yuppie eighties, the neoliberal nineties passed you by. You Wayne and Cheryl are sixties counterculture freaks. You are survivors—more than survivors, you are fighters. You are real activists. You write letters to politicians. You are not just working in the education program for the money and the influence; you are both very firm in your dedication to education. You fight causes. You have a mission.

When in 1985 the prison services discovered that they had three HIV-positive inmates, they segregated them. When you Wayne heard that Diane Darling was in the AIDS unit, you went to the high ranker in the jail and asked if you could go in there and talk to her. They said No, that they wouldn't have people going back and forth. But you insisted. Finally they let you go in. You told her that if she ever needed to talk, or cry, or scream, you would be there. Six months later Head Office started what they called the AIDS Task Force—a group of civilians to enter the jail to educate inmates about HIV. They appointed you the first AIDS peer educator. You and Cheryl ran the HIV-AIDS and hepatitis C committee for almost six years. Every year you put on a different event for World AIDS Day.

Your old crony Ashleigh from the King's Cross cabarets got herself arrested and with you Cheryl organized the Long Bay Cowgirls. You sewed up an extravagant, theatrical frock for yourself.

It's with the other transsexuals that you Cheryl are having your own way in something. You give a lot of support to those who end up in the jail. One who was sinking rapidly had a great fear of dying alone. How envious she was of you and Wayne who will die together. You accompanied her all the way while she was going no where; you were there when she died, you were with her.

No police force could hope to prosecute and incarcerate all thieves, addicts, and perverts. Every convict is an expiatory sacrifice who suffers his or her life for all.

In heading off to the back alleys and wastelands where our heads are exposed to the blows of chance we know in exhilaration what we have received by chance, what we are by chance. Love is abruptly ignited in impasses and traps; it is the combustion of interpenetrating dreams of bodies collapsed and dysfunctional. It is the incandescence of luck in the most squalid, the most sordid circumstances, the worst luck.

Shit happens. You Wayne and Cheryl have been HIV-positive for ten years. You Wayne were stabbed with a needle by a patient while you were a sweeper in the clinic. A few weeks later you Cheryl were hospitalized with anorexia; in the middle of the night two men who were HIV-positive raped you. About the same time you both contracted hepatitis C. For the past eighteen months you Wayne have full-blown AIDS symptoms. You have bowel cancer. Shit happens. In 1993 you had come down with so many opportunistic infections

Cheryl they gave you at best six months to live. Then they discovered that the virus was replicating not in your blood but in your bone marrow. There was only one other such case reported—in the United States. Shit happens.

You Wayne have a chest infection. Your skin is breaking out with Kaposi's sarcoma scabs. The ones that are on your backside, it's like sitting on boils. When you take off your underpants for the night, it rips the scabs stuck to them. You Wayne and you Cheryl take everything very methodically: We will have to deal with this, you say. And then, later, you say, We will have to deal with that. You each day defy the plague. You are very courageous. You savor each day you are alive. The level of energy you produce is a manifestation of your will. You keep each other alive. You Cheryl say, Whatever keeps us together even twenty-four hours. Even one hour. You are allowed to see a prison doctor every five weeks. You Wayne said to him, Listen, I will keep myself alive whilever Cheryl needs me. I will not allow myself to die whilever Cheryl needs me. I don't need your drugs to do that. I have the will in me, the love that I have for Cheryl in me, to keep myself alive whilever Cheryl needs me. But everybody knows the moment one of you dies, you'll both die.

When you get sick Wayne you see how it affects Cheryl: she hates to see you sick. That makes you feel guilty, because it really worries her. Quite often you'd be sick, and you'd try not to show it, for Cheryl's benefit. But then you chastise yourself, because the biggest and the best part of your relationship you think is the honesty. And you think, Well, if I try and hide it from Cheryl then I'm not being honest with her. But sometimes you think, Well, maybe she doesn't need to know. She just had a bad deal today. But then you think that if you knew that Cheryl was feeling this bad and didn't tell you, you'd be very upset with her. It's a big thing with you, honesty.

You Wayne protect Cheryl. A lot of people think that no one'll touch Cheryl, no one'll rape Cheryl because she's got

AIDS. But there are blokes who think they can't get AIDS from Cheryl giving them head. Some think that unless they ejaculate inside her, they are at no risk. There are those who think there is no risk if they use a condom. But a number of people have approached you over the months and asked you for your blood! Some blokes want our blood, you say, because they believe if they get AIDS it can help them get out of jail a little bit earlier. Some believe that it can at least help them get some privileges. Some blokes want our blood because they want to commit suicide. Others want to square up on somebody they don't like. Most times you Wayne take him aside and say, Fuck off! Never ask me that again! But with a close friend, it's not that simple. One said, Come off, Wayne, you're playing God with my life.

Cancers, putrescent infections, blindness, madness, agonizing pain await people dying of AIDS. Those who care for them, those who love them leave their bedside, to go to the other room to get food, to answer the telephone, to receive visitors, they go out to buy groceries and do the laundry. They can, when they can no longer endure to keep watch, slip out of the room. They are not locked in a six-by-ten-foot cement cell all the weeks and hours, all the days and the nights of the infections, the despair, the agony, the delirium, the dying.

In taking our ambitions, our values, and our achievements seriously we turn ourselves into idols, which we cannot help fearing will soon be covered with graffiti and pigeon shit. What else can we do, do we do, but laugh when we think we got born though nobody wanted us, when we think they have to pay to keep us alive here because we robbed them, when we open our eyes to find our cell buzzing with the pompous assertiveness of a bumblebee, when a frolicsome mouse chooses to give birth to her babies in Long Bay gaol?

The two men who raped you Cheryl are both dead now. May they rest in peace, you say. You went to the funeral service for them. Forgive and forget, you say. Just forget, you say.

One would have to remember and forgive everything, from the day you were born and abandoned. Cheryl cannot change who she is, you Wayne say. It's one of the things you love so much about her.

Love attaches to the abyss. It is hate that circumscribes its own identity. Tell me whom you hate and I will tell you who you are. Tell me whom you love and I will know as little about you as before.

How lucky I am! you Cheryl think. How lucky I have been! How lucky to have met Wayne. How lucky not to die alone, like the other transvestites. How lucky to have quality life. The level of energy you keep up is the energy of this defiance and exhilaration.

One day an old flame of yours, Cheryl, appeared in the prison. For weeks how anguished you were—there had now suddenly appeared to you one last chance to know a great passion before you die. Although you realized that leaving Wayne would kill him, Wayne said nothing whatever about what he quickly understood was going on. Then you understood that your great passion made of violence, adoration, and lust is Wayne.

And then one day the prison authorities summoned you Cheryl and presented you with your release. You were led back to the cell, you packed your green prison clothes in a state of pounding agitation. The gates of Long Bay gaol closed behind you.

They gave you a small sum of money; it was not enough to buy a real gun. You took a perfume bottle, practiced holding it in your hand wrapped in a scarf. You went to the McDonald's a little after midday; you handed the cashier a piece of paper on which you had written: "This is a hold-up. Give me $200." On the back of the paper you had written your name, your address, your phone number, your jail number. And "P.S. Don't call until 9:30; I won't be ready." By midnight you were back with Wayne. You tell him how, shrieking with drag queen laughter.

IV

Understanding

*I*STANBUL SPANS THE THREE PROMONTORIES converging at the entry of the Bosporus into the Sea of Marmara. They have risen ever higher as earth and rubble accumulated on them, as Semistra founded by Thracians some thousand years BCE was supplanted in 657 BCE by Byzantion, which was occupied by settlers from Argos and Megara, later conquered by the Persians and then by the Spartans and finally by the Romans under Septimius Severus, and rebuilt by Constantine. The city held three and a half million people when I first visited it; now it has expanded to hold eleven million. The first summer after I finished my studies I spent in Istanbul; a few years later I spent another summer there, tracking down excavations where ever older layers of the city have been unearthed. Going again now was a return back through my own history. But this time I only wanted to see again the Hagia Sophia.

When in 330 CE the emperor Constantine transferred the capital of the Roman Empire to Byzantium, his intention was to maintain and preserve the Roman world by transferring the seat of its government from the Italian peninsula, then prey to barbarians, to the stronghold on the Bosporus. And it was a Roman city, citadel of the Roman order, that Constantine laid out over the ancient town of Byzantium; he named it Nova Roma. He located seven hills and walled them in with a formidable circle of land and sea walls. Its avenues met the imperial concourse at the city gates and led to the Hippodrome; they were laid out for triumphant military processions. They were broad and monumental, flanked on either side by colonnades, covered porticoes and ambulatories that went on for miles, where the people of the capital came to watch their imperial existence on parade. Behind these porticoes there extended the markets in which the wares and booty of a vast Mediterranean empire were laid out and circulated. The center of the imperial city was the Hippodrome; all the imperial palaces and administrative buildings were directly connected with it. In the Hippodrome the imperial army trained and exhibited its might. In the Hippodrome the people of the capital assembled to celebrate imperial life in chariot races, gladiatorial contests, and triumphal parades. All the principal gods were enshrined in the Hippodrome and all the conquered gods were set up there (Constantine converted to Christianity only on his deathbed). Civil wars were fomented by insurrectional military factions in the barracks of the Hippodrome to be won or lost in the huge public assemblages during which this people restructured, reversed, and renewed its civic existence.

In 532 Constantine's church, the Megale Ekklesia, was burned by the Nika uprising. Justinian put down the uprising with the slaughter of forty thousand insurgents in the Hippodrome. Just six weeks later he launched construction of what was to be the great church of the empire. It was completed and consecrated in less than six years.

This building, the Hagia Sophia, inaugurated the Byzantine world. Here was born the Byzantine nocturnal spirituality, its processionals through the city at dusk in gilded vestments and clouds of incense, its sacred ceremonies and rituals taking place from sunset to sunrise, its lavish and sensual expression of religion in sumptuous garments, mosaic visions of precious stone, burnished iconography in which the severe and persecuted simplicity of the Semitic religion of the carpenter's son became voluptuous and mystical—a religion not of the cross and the redemption of sins but of Easter and the glorification of the body (each Sunday, Byzantine Christianity celebrates not the Lord's Supper and the communion before Gethsemane, but the resurrection of the dead Christ). This religion, with its incantatory, liturgical, and kerygmatic theology that never became rationalized doctrine as in the West, was a sacralization of mystery, of the cloud of unknowing in the sanctuary concealed behind iconostases, of rapturous states of soul. In this Christianity sacralization is not moralization and not spiritualization but redemptive transfiguration.

Romans came here to build, in the East, a Nova Roma, but with the erection of the Hagia Sophia the New Rome became the New Jerusalem. Heaven is a city, and the Lord of heavens assumes the functions of the civic powers. Conversely the city is a heaven. With its hills, processional ways, groves, and courtyards, it is the mirror image of the heavenly Jerusalem. And at its center is the Hagia Sophia, the temple of the Holy Wisdom from which everything emanates and from which everything is ordered and ordained.

This the emperor's basilica was also the center of Byzantine imperialism; it was here that power was invested with divine authority, that the sacred emperor, the basileus, governed by pronouncing decrees under the celestial vault. The public life of each Byzantine subject is enacted in the person of the basileus. Each one is glorified by participating in the transcendent existence of the sacred ruler.

I climbed up the promontory of old Stamboul: there on the height it stands. I see massive piers and buttresses, the waves of metal-roofed domes and half domes on top, no decoration or outlining of individual forms, and a confusion of crumbling structures at its base: a mountain.

I enter between two of these piers, the Imperial Portal, the facade framing it long gone. I find myself in the exonarthex, a shallow hall extending on both sides with cross-vaulted ceiling, its bared and crumbled bricks like some ancient ruin. I advance into the narthex, broader, with gilt mosaics on its domed ceiling and, above the southwest entrance, a mosaic picture of Constantine offering a model of his city and Justinian a model of his basilica to the Queen of Heaven.

I pass through the central portal. For a thousand years this basilica was the biggest building on the planet. But as I go in my breath is taken away: it floats! The supports, the lines of thrust and counterthrust, the fall of the weight and its elevation upon piers and pillars are invisible; all that occurs outside. At once my eyes are drawn to the fabled dome, mosaicked in gold ribs, suspended over forty windows.

> There, overhead, looming vast in the shadowy air,
> Arches the rounded helm of the heavenly house,
> Like unto the burnished roof of heaven,

wrote Paul the Silentiary, who watched its construction.

From the dome my gaze is sent in arcs and half arcs to the rhythm of billowing half domes and conchs below it. The descending lines of those arcs merge into the lines of the upper walls and the arcades, then cross the leafy capitals to the arcades below them. The whole logic of forms, of domes and half domes, conchs and arcs, galleries and windows is commanded from, and derives from, the dome. Below the dome suspended over forty windows, floating over light, the edifice like a bell barely grazes the earth with its shadows.

My eyes travel the half domes, conchs, and arcades without seeing junctures where force and thrust are countered by mass and counterthrust. Vaults and arches mold the space only along their edges, describing a rhythm of lines. Where the descending lines of domes and arches meet rising vertical lines, there are double braids of sculptured lace introducing air and emptiness. The corners of the basilica split to open back upon barrel cylinders required by their domes above. I do not see massive piles to support the dome; I see only side walls on which twin

marble slabs, whose veinings mirror one another, bordered
by richly ornamental bands, serrated reglets, and the vertical
rectangles placed over broad plaques and narrower horizon-
tal bands, turn the mass of piers and walls into planes. The
walls break into double-storied arcades, becoming transparent
with the great windows behind them. Their slender columns
that do not taper and whose capitals are baskets of acanthus
leaves turn the arcades into latticework rather than structural
supports. "This structure seems not to rest on solid masonry,"
Procopius of Caesarea wrote in the year 555, "but to hover over
space with its golden dome suspended from heaven. All these
details, fitted together with incredible skill in mid-air and
floating off from each other and resting only on the parts next
to them, produce a single and most extraordinary harmony in
the work, and yet do not permit the spectator to linger much
over the study of any one of them, but each detail attracts the
eye and draws it on irresistibly to itself, so that the vision shifts
continually in sweeping circles."[1] The mountain of stone seen
outside is, inside, dematerialized; mass and weight lose their
reality here; materiality becomes superficial.

Streams of sunlight enter through the upper walls of glass
and hundreds of arched windows; they overlap and cross to
intensify: the inside of this mountain is a fountain of tinted
light. Light glows on the sheets of veined polychrome marble
of the walls. The domes, half domes, conchs, and vaulted
ceilings behind the arcades are covered with mosaic; made of
tiny cubes of translucent glass with gold leaf inside, reflecting
light in all directions, mosaic does not gleam, it shimmers.
The designs made of gold, silver, red, green, and blue glass
tesserae are nonrepresentational; they relay on the surfaces of
the vaults the lines of their edges. The surfaces of the walls are
thus vibrant with an interior luminosity; they do not enclose
but irradiate.

The side walls, transparent between the latticework of the

arcades, do not enclose the central space but render it indeterminate. The Hagia Sophia works a negation of materiality in
the apotheosis of space—a vast radiant space without precise
frontiers, whose glowing surfaces do not bound it. The longer
the visitor remains in this lambent space, the more the impression of immensity intensifies until he has the impression
that it is the heavenly vaults that hover above him. The Hagia
Sophia gives a vision of the destiny of all that is terrestrial to
be redeemed, glorified; it is matter being transfigured into
shimmering light and splendor.

"Praise and worship to the Almighty who held me worthy
to complete such a work," Justinian exclaimed in wonder when
it was consecrated. "Solomon, I have outdone thee!"

In 1203 the Crusaders under Boniface of Monferrat and
Doge Enrico Dandolo of Venice broke through the sea walls
and sacked Constantinople. They looted the Hagia Sophia,
enthroning a harlot in the patriarch's throne to sing bawdy
songs and insult Orthodoxy. Then they reconsecrated it to
Latin Christianity. In 1453 the Ottoman armies broke through
the land walls, and twenty-one-year-old Sultan Mehmet II
mounted a mule and rode directly to the Hagia Sophia, dis-
mounted and fell to his knees, sprinkling a handful of earth
over his turban in a gesture of humility. He ordered that the
church be immediately converted to Islamic worship under the
name of Aya Sofya Camii Kabir and that a minaret be raised.
In 1923, after defeating the post–World War I Greek occupation, Mustafa Kemal Pasha, Atatürk, terminated worship in
the mosque and converted it into a museum. Of the Byzantine
Empire nothing remains; of the Ottoman Empire there is only
left the fragment called Turkey, exhausting its resources in the
savage oppression of the Kurdish independence struggle in
its eastern provinces. Of all wars and slaughters, the laws and
administration, the emperors and the heroes of their battles
acclaimed and covered with glory, the religions that ruled

here, there remains today only the building itself, which has survived more than a thousand earthquakes.

It looked like the end of the world. The low mountains about Qal'at Sam'an in northern Syria are visibly ancient; one does not see the cross sections of rock strata; their surfaces are broken rocks worn smooth that do not retain pockets of soil. The skies are empty of birds, even of vultures. With nothing to retain the gaze, one's eyes contemplate a spectacle of awesome desolation exposed to the harsh radiation of the sun. Rare shepherds tend small flocks of sheep and goats grazing scrub bushes on the bottom of the mountain folds. One is pained to contemplate the desperation of their lives.

It must have been sheep and goats that denuded the mountains when their trees were burned during various Byzantine military campaigns against Persian and then Arab invaders. For I had passed the ruins of abandoned cities in the region. The valleys had once had flourishing orchards and vineyards.

On top of the highest mountain, I come upon an old man seated on a rock before a massive stone wall. He is bald, his face leathered by the sun, his body still full and sturdy. He hails me with a broad smile. He tells me his name is Mustafa. He speaks ungrammatical but understandable English. He is the guardian of this place. He has guarded it for forty-nine years now. He lives in the valley below. When he was young he climbed the thirteen kilometers each way on foot. Now on bad days his arthritis flares; an acquaintance with a truck brings him here. He has had but two years of education as a boy, in a Koranic school. But he knows well the story of this place. I sit down on another rock, and he reaches for a kettle of water, puts a large pinch of mint leaves in it, and sets it to boil on the charcoal embers of a clay brazier.

Somewhere around 400 of the Common Era, Mustafa tells me, a shepherd wandered down here from Cilicia in what is now southern Turkey, with his son Simon. Simon, it is known, was born in 392. When he was thirteen years old Simon entered a monastery in the town of Heliodorus and in ten years became a priest. But it was not a wish to escape the harsh barrenness of the shepherd's life that led him to take refuge in the monastery, for he found the life there too comfortable and transferred to another monastery in Telanissos with a reputation for greater rigor. In fact monasteries were also refuges for fugitives from military service, the burdens of taxes, and debt. In the Telanissos monastery Simon practiced such austerities that the abbot judged him incompatible with the community of brothers and asked him to leave. He ascended the highest peak in the region, shifted a great rock and climbed up on it to stand gazing at the heavens. Kindly shepherds began bringing him humble nourishment and listened spellbound as he lifted their eyes from the daily hunt for the means of survival to cosmic regions. Before long more and more pious people began climbing the mountain to hear him speak and to touch the hem of his garment. Annoyed, he, with the help of some shepherds, hoisted another rock on top of the first, so that they could no longer touch him. But the people kept coming. There was no escaping them by fleeing his mountain to the valleys below; he kept adding another rock to his pillar until it reached forty meters. He had lived thirty-nine years on top of a pillar when he died in 459, at the age of sixty-seven.

The kettle is boiling; Mustafa pours out two cups of mint tea and offers one to me. He continues. Simon's fame had reached Constantinople; the basileus sent priests to bring his body in procession to be buried in the Hagia Sophia. Seventeen years later, the basileus Leo and then Zenon ordered the construction of a basilica around Simon's pillar. Eventually five hundred monks lived and worshipped in a monastery built next to the basilica. In the ninth century the Byzantine armies launched a counteroffensive against the Arab invaders and fortified this site with massive stone ramparts. The monks were replaced with soldiers. In 986 the region fell to the Arabs, but the basilica was spared and Orthodox priests were allowed to return and resume their rites. Earthquakes shook the basilica repeatedly, and in the fifteenth century it was finally abandoned.

Mustafa takes out a sheet of paper from the pocket of his robe and shows me five diagrams: the Byzantine cross, the Latin cross, the Coptic cross, the Nestorian cross—and a circle with a cross over it: the sun named Baal worshipped by the Syrian pagans. He tells me to look for them on the now fallen columns of the basilica built about Simon's pillar.

I advance through the iron gate in the massive fortress wall and climb under gnarled old trees to the summit, which extends in a flat shady plaza. On one end there is a large stone building whose walls are cracked and roof collapsed. On the other end I am astonished to see the basilica: laid out in a cross with whole chunks of its walls still standing, the carved portal frame of its facade intact with an elegant stone arch across it. In the center a shapeless rock some five feet high: what is left of Simon's pillar.

I search on the fallen rocks till I find each of the five crosses the basileus's men carved into pillars and portals. Then I walk around the crest of the long useless ramparts whose great ashlars were too heavy for the villagers below to haul down for their modest buildings. The sky is cloudless, the thin air serene. My gaze opens upon vast distances below, drifting over the cockled mountains covered with rocks that were left when the continental plate buckled eons ago.

Standing there, I contemplate the lives of the shepherds who still wander these mountains, whose desperation can allow them no space to harbor thoughts but those driven by hunger. How could one like them have his eyes so opened to cosmic dimensions that he could only live perched on an eagle crag! And how strange that this shepherd who only wanted to flee the traffic of men became renowned throughout Christendom and beyond.

The basileuses Leo and Zenon misunderstood him. They

took his body that longed to separate itself from the crowds of disciples and put it in the imperial church of the great metropolis. They took him to be a Christian saint, but he no more found in the gospel told in Palestine the forces that drove him to a pillar he built on the highest mountain than the basileuses found in it the constitution for the imperial Christendom over which they reigned.

Simon's voice has not been heard here for almost sixteen hundred years, and he has left no written message for me to read. I am the only visitor to the site this afternoon, and were there pilgrims and processions of Orthodox or Latin, Coptic or Nestorian, or pagan priests here, I would grasp little of, and be able to give less credence to, their creeds and theologies. This site is no longer a monastery but a Syrian state museum. The local people, Muslims, call it Qal'at Sam'an, Simon's Fortress, and indeed it is the massive, still intact walls, built in the ninth century to secure the Byzantine assault into the encroaching Arab kingdom, that you see from the valleys below. But that is another misunderstanding of this place.

Today psychoanalysis sets aside the extravagances and private myths of the past and leads the deluded to the sanity of a mind assured of the truth of scientific materialism. It would look for drives in Simon's personal history that had knotted into such extreme sociopathic and megalomaniac compulsions. Now I too am on the summit of this mountain thrust high in the pellucid sky, seeing the vast desolate earth below, its sinister armies, their hatreds, devastations, pillage, and tortures having passed on or clashing still in remote enclaves we call civilization. I am transfixed by the sight of Simon's pillar, now reduced to a single shapeless huge rock by, Mustafa told me, countless pilgrims who had chipped pieces to carry away as relics and amulets for their magic power. I too feel the magic of that rock, and of the summit of this mountain. I hear the murmur of psychoanalysts in my head. But how could a life supported on the absolute materiality of stone, eyes open to vast spaces by the radiant transparency of the skies, be living in a closed private space of his illusions; how could such a life be mad?

Imperceptibly the sun was descending. The light grew softer. Then the sun's rays passed under the trees about me and touched Simon's rock, which glowed with ochre serenity. Below, the mountains began to drift in gentle twilight and slowly subsided into darkness. I scrambled down to the gate; it was time for Mustafa to be on his way. He smiled; he had the teacups ready. We sipped the tea in silence. I felt no urge to leave.

The builders of the Aya Sophia, unbeknownst to themselves, brought out the glory that resides in stone and light. Simon lived in that glory for thirty-nine years. Across all the noncommunication of Byzantine theological intellectualism and a shepherd's enigmas, across all the kilometers of battlefields between them where armies fought for ethnic identity and for ideas, did they not understand one another?

The Dreadful Mystic Banquet

*I*N KATHMANDU I had to buy a package tour to get a visa for Tibet; I bought the three-day package. The air hostess pointed out the mountain that British imperialists named Mount Everest and that the Tibetans call Chomolungma— Goddess Mother of the Snows. The passengers held up their cameras, working their zoom lenses to catch sight of mountain-climbing teams. The airport is seventy-five kilometers from Lhasa; during the drive down the modern highway, crossing new bridges, I realized: the Chinese will never leave Tibet. We were put up at the Holiday Inn and served dinner in the restaurant. The menu here on top of the world was ten pages of international, Chinese, and Tibetan cuisine. The wine list offered Chinese, French, Australian, and Californian wines.

We had a silent Tibetan driver and a Chinese guide. Lhasa had been a pilgrimage center, not a true urban center; its preinvasion population was only 25,000. Now it is a city of 250,000, extending along new avenues lined with apartment complexes, supermarkets, department stores, automobile showrooms, warehouses, and machine shops, whose fronts are covered with sheets of enameled metal and identified with neon signs. A great square has been opened up in front of the Potala, the former palace of the Dalai Lama; on its sides are a giant department store, a restaurant, and a disco. The guide extended our vision of the modern metropolis with verbal pictures of industries producing basic and high-tech industrial products; she itemized at length the consumer goods now available in the department stores and supermarkets. We were taken to the Potala, where we filed down the aisles of the few dozen restored rooms of the thousand rooms the palace contains, viewing giant gold statues of the Buddha, and to the Summer Palace of the Dalai Lama, built in 1956 and furnished, our guide pointed out, like a palace of a raja in British India. We were given time to wander among the shops at the gate selling thangkas, sacred paintings, from the palace and monasteries. I saw two skull bowls, one lined inside with silver. The guide came over to tell me that in feudal Tibet rebellious peasants were decapitated and the tops of their skulls were used as bowls in the banquets of the monks. I bought the skull bowls. The next tour she would not have occasion to illustrate with them the vision of the barbarous regime the Chinese had supplanted.

At the end of the three days, I packed my bags and slipped out to find a hotel in the old city and stayed on. Only a few blocks of old Lhasa remain, around the Jokhang, the great temple. Here the houses are built of stone, three or four stories high, with intricately carved wood window frames. The Jokhang was crowded at all times of the day; Tibetans were circling the temple by making complex full-length prostrations. I had read that in old Tibet pilgrims came to Lhasa from great distances this way: standing, making the complex salutation, then extending their body full-length to the ground, rising and stepping one body length ahead, and making another prostration. I wandered in the market that surrounds the Jokhang; there were piles of vegetables, yak butter, handwoven traditional Tibetan clothes, prayer wheels, and prayer flags. Some men wore their long hair coiled about their heads with bright red wool threads woven into them; these are Khambas, nomads from the East, who had waged a hopeless armed resistance to the Chinese invasion in 1959. I looked into their eyes wondering what Tibet they saw; they did not meet my gaze but looked away. I stood long before the Jokhang watching the pilgrims whose eyes did not look at the surrounding market and me but were possessed by another vision.

In my hotel room I contemplated the skull bowls I had purchased. The hotelkeeper told me that in old Tibet, on this high plateau where permafrost and the lack of trees make burial and cremation impossible, the Tibetans took the bodies of the dead to a height above the city and there dismembered the corpses and cut them into small pieces to leave them to the eagles. They called it sky burial. Lamas who had led exemplary lives on their deathbed willed their skulls to be cut into bowls and given to young lamas to be used as begging bowls when they went on pilgrimage.

Seeing is believing; we cannot make ourselves really doubt that the visible, tangible, audible world about us is real. But we also speak of "seeing things" that are illusory. Do we have a set of criteria and procedures to identify and dispel illusions? In fact, we recognize illusions by continuing to look at what is visible. The visual field, philosopher Maurice Merleau-Ponty pointed out, of itself separates out really visible things from memories and images, which do not settle in among the really visible things but haunt them.[1] The water on the road ahead dissipates into a sheen of light when we get closer and see better. The dead lover we catch sight of in the crowd leaving the cemetery subsides into the settled features of a stranger when we approach.

What is the vision of visionaries, of seers? That of the *Gilgamesh* and the *Mahabharata,* the *Odyssey* and the *Ring of the Nibelungen*? That of Plotinus and Saint John of the Cross? The visions of Dante, William Blake, and James Joyce? The visions of Simón Bolívar, Che Guevara, and Nelson Mandela?

Anthropologists take the visions recounted in myths and legends of a culture as symbolic mappings of the environment and the institutions of a people. The vision is interpreted as a constellation of symbols, each materializing a connection or relationship. Claude Lévi-Strauss and Jacques Lacan said that the eccentric images of individual fantasy constitute a private myth.[2] In his "fantasy space" that psychotherapists scrutinize, that individual works to fill in, with meaningful symbols, the gap between the universal meanings of the public myth—or, today, of science—and the particularities of his own situation.

To separate the vision of visionaries from delusions, our philosophers of knowledge invoke meaning. What the vision presents is not what is there and seeable; instead it anchors meanings in visualized heroes, demigods, and demons. Our epistemology admits that the vision can well be more meaningful than what is given to perceptual sight and more meaningful than what can be represented in the universal and abstract terms of a conceptual diagram or mapping.[3]

But the concepts of meaning and symbol can only misconstrue the visions of visionaries. A visionary is not constructing a system of symbols, and it is not by interpreting its meanings that a vision takes hold. The genuineness of a vision is not the result of a procedure of criticism and verification. The most skeptical epistemologist does not marshal a set of criteria to authenticate the visions of the *Iliad,* the Song of Solomon, or Mahatma Gandhi. The visions of visionaries of themselves will separate from delusions by settling into the course of the world. We acknowledge them by finding them extending the paths and the horizons of our lives.

Does not every vision involve great risk for the visionary? Scholars who interpret the visions of epic poets and religious writers do not make us feel the risks involved; perhaps they themselves feel no worse risks than peer neglect in academia. The psychoanalysis of literature and art has brought into discredit the search for the sources of Milton's and Joyce's visions in their psychopathology. But with that discredit, we have neglected the effects of their visions on them—and on us. The vision of visionaries dazzles, blinds, wounds.

Alexandra David-Neel tells of a rite practiced in old Tibet called *chöd*, which she had witnessed and into which she herself had been partially initiated.[4] It is a kind of mystery play with one actor only, the celebrant. It has been devised to so terrify the participants that one hears of men who have suddenly gone mad or fallen dead while engaged in its performance.

The one to perform *chöd*, the *naljorpa*, must have long perfected the ritual dance to be performed, his steps forming geometrical figures, turnings on one foot, stamping and leaping in time with the liturgic recitation. He must have mastered ringing the *dorjee*, a bell, wielding the *phurba*, a magic dagger, beating the *damaru*, a small drum, and sounding the *kangling*, a trumpet made of a human bone. The dancers are young ascetics emaciated by austerities, clad in ragged robes, their unwashed faces lit by hard, resolute, ecstatic eyes.

The rite is performed in a cemetery or any wild site that awakens feelings of terror. The place is thought the more suitable if it is associated with a terrible legend or if a tragic event has actually occurred there recently. The rite is designed to call up the occult forces or conscious beings that may exist in such places, generated either by actual deeds or by the concentration of many people's thoughts of imagined events.

The ceremony begins with long mystic preliminaries during which the celebrant tramples down all passions and his selfishness. Then the celebrant blows his bone trumpet, calling the hungry demons to the feast he intends to lay before them. Suddenly he sees a female deity, who springs from the top of his head—from his own will—and stands before him, sword in hand. With one stroke of her sword she severs the head of the *naljorpa*. With further strokes she rips open his belly and dismembers and skins him. Troops of ghouls appear and close in for the feast.

The blood gushes forth, the body's internal organs lie exposed, and the monstrous guests snarl, bite, and chew, while the celebrant excites them and urges them on, chanting the liturgic words of unreserved surrender:

> For ages, in the course of renewed births I have borrowed from countless living beings—at the cost of their welfare and life—food, clothing, all kinds of services to sustain my body, to keep it in comfort and to defend it against death. Today, I pay my debt, offering for destruction this body which I have held so dear. I give my flesh to the hungry, my blood to the thirsty, my skin to clothe those who are naked, my bones as fuel to those who suffer from cold. I give my happiness to the unhappy ones. I give my breath to bring back the dying to life. Shame on me if I shrink from giving my *self*! Shame on you, wretched demoniac beings, if you do not dare to prey upon it.[5]

This act of the "Mystery" is called the red meal. If the initiate is one far advanced, it will be followed by the black meal. The vision of the demoniac banquet vanishes, the laughter and cries of the ghouls die away. Utter loneliness in a gloomy landscape succeeds the orgy of ghouls, and the exaltation aroused in the *naljorpa* by his dramatic sacrifice subsides. Now he sees himself having become a small heap of charred human bones that lie on a lake of black mud—the mud of misery, of moral defilement, and of harmful deeds in which he has cooperated during the course of numberless lives whose origin is lost in the night of time. He sees that the very idea of sacrifice is but an illusion, an offshoot of blind, groundless pride. In fact, he has nothing to give away, because he is nothing. What does it matter if these useless bones sink into the muddy lake! This silent renunciation of the ascetic who realizes that he holds nothing that he can renounce, and who utterly relin-

quishes the elation springing from the idea of sacrifice, closes
the rite.

In the *chöd* all things that the celebrant has perceived, understood, and used as means and nutrients are seen in a wild
phantasmal form of pure consuming mouths, now consuming
the celebrant. There is not the utterance of a new discourse,
imbued with a higher meaning. What the vision stages is not
a revelation of sovereign, cosmic, or sacred meaning but the
potlatch of meaning in the demented cries and the laughter
of the ghouls. There are words, but they are the liturgic words
of unreserved surrender with which the celebrant excites the
ghouls that are devouring his dismembered body and urges
them on.

The celebrant does not experience the dismemberment
and devouring of his substance in terror and pain but in
ecstatic exultation. He experiences all the fullness and riches
of his being as a plenitude that restores, heals, and nourishes
innumerable alien species. He experiences this plenitude in
the ecstatic giving of all his substance to them. For every
ecstasy is an expropriation, a release of excess forces without
recompense.

The vision does not culminate in the transfiguration and
glorification of the visionary; it closes with the ascetic's silent
renunciation. The *chöd* celebrates the extremism of magna-
nimity, a gratitude that gives without limit, the extremism
of renunciation, renouncing even the wild exultation of this
expropriation.

This vision haunts us too because our sight of the working
world about us is today doubled by a cosmic vision, supplied to
us not by monks but by our scientists.[6] Our sciences and technology long served our vision of ourselves as demiurgic and
Promethean agents and as cosmic legislators, obeying only laws
of our own making. Today our science shows us that deforestation, monoculture, cattle rearing, damming of rivers, irrigation,

pesticides, and genetic engineering of crop species are devastating the planet's biodiversity and polluting the topsoil, the water table, and the oceans. Ecological science shows us to be one species in a complex planetary ecosystem, unable ourselves to survive without countless other species thriving. Microbiology discovers that the first celled organisms developed as one species of microbe entered into symbiosis with another. The chloroplasts and mitochondria, the oxygen-processing cellular energy-producers in plants and animals, were originally independent cyanobacteria and proteobacteria that came to live inside the cells that eventually conjoined into plants and animals. Six hundred species of anaerobic bacteria live in our mouths, neutralizing the toxins that all plants produce to ward off their enemies; in our intestines live four hundred species, without which we could not digest and absorb the food we ingest. Ecological science and evolutionary biology confront us with a vision in which our species is but one avatar of microbe evolution, our individuality but an abstract figure floating over swarmings and symbioses.

What a disconnect there is today between our visions and our lives! We have let go of the old anthropocentric myths and stoically accepted as true the astronomer's vision of the vast empty spaces and finite time of the whole universe. We have let go of the Edenic myths that represented all species as created for our use and consumption. But our economic and political life is engineered and fine-tuned for continual production, using the sciences for domination over want, hunger, disease, discomfort, and even death.

The *chöd* in old Tibet is a ritual, not only a vision. The ritual is a concentrated form of many actions that will be performed consequent upon the vision. We no longer bless our meals or lose our individualism in carnivals—our modern culture has demythologized and commercialized collective rituals from our own feudal and theocratic past and psychopathologized individual rituals. Yet is not our life full of rituals that restage the anthropocentric and predatory vision? Hunting, spectator sports, and extreme sports are participationist visions of transfigured vitality, glorified power, and skill, of a triumphant animal species. There are rituals of consumption: banquets, balls, haute couture fashion shows, yachts, casinos. Haute cuisine is the high mass of our global civilization. In traveling from country to country, being served like the emperor in restaurants where any substance, any plant or animal, is laid out for our consumption, we situate ourselves in the food chain at the top. We alone are the uneaten ones, the unexchangeable value, the cosmic dignity. We have buried our corpses out of the reach of scavenger animals, dogs and hyenas; have encased them in stone mausoleums and steel coffins; have mummified them and have injected them with formaldehyde so that they will not be food of larvae or cremated them to make them inedible even to bacteria.

We do not have visions that activate the compulsion of one to whom so much was given to give in turn. We do not have in our culture rituals to conduct initiates into the exultation of giving oneself. What rituals will we have to contrive, to celebrate in elemental spaces, in order that the visions with which our ecological and evolutionary biology and our astronomy today confront us may enter into our lives?

The Return of Extinct Religions

I WENT TO MONGOLIA for the New Year's Day of the new
millennium. In a shop attached to the State Museum in
Ulaanbaatar I came upon a ritual horn that I immediately saw
was a human femur bone, very aged, wrapped in now fragile
silk bands. Then in a shop attached to the former grand lama's
summer palace, now also a museum, I found another. In each
shop, with signs and gestures and the words "Mongolia" and
"America," I asked, if I purchased this could I take it out of the
country? The shopkeepers spoke no English, but wrote out slips
in Mongolian script and indicated with smiles and gestures
that those would clear them at the airport.

At the airport X-ray, a short sturdy woman in official uniform came over and said politely, "Excuse me, but do you have
bones in your suitcase?" I opened the suitcase, pulled them
out and showed her the slips from the shops. "But," she said,
"these are only sales slips. You should have gotten permission
from the Ministry of Cultural Affairs." She was troubled by
the sales price on the slips—fifty dollars for the one, seventy
dollars for the other. In fact I had been quite willing to lose
that if, as I had suspected, they were illegal to export. But for
her, fifty dollars represented an exorbitant sum—a month's
salary for a government official. She asked me what I was
doing in Mongolia. I took pleasure in answering, "I'm a tourist!" for I had been the only guest in the hotel and had not

seen any other tourist in midwinter Ulaanbaatar. She told me to check in and went to consult another official, an old man, no doubt a scholar of the old Mongolian culture. After I had checked in, she came to say that I could keep them. But at the second X-ray machine for carry-on bags, the officials, young and educated and secular, visibly disliked my permission to carry out these evidences of the old, superstitious, and barbaric Mongolia.

These two hollowed-out human femur bones are clearly ritual horns, but I have not dared to blow them to hear their sound. I had seen only one in the displays of the National Museum of Mongolian History, with its identification only in Mongolian. The books I have consulted give contradictory identifications. According to some, they are ritual objects from the primal shamanist religion of the Mongols, bones taken from virgin women who were sacrificed. According to others, they are bones of holy Buddhist monks donated by them on their deathbeds for temple use. I could not help thinking the latter might be the sanitized version for our times and for tourists.

I then could not determine the processions and the rites in which these human bones figured, and can recover no after-image of the titanic or demonic figures that appeared in the visions and trances of Mongolian religions. An anthropologist or a historiographer could conclude that I can know nothing of the nature of these objects.

Yet are they not sacred (Latin *sacrum,* separated) in the very absence of the ritual and ceremonial cult in which they figured? Separated irrevocably from their ritual use, they are also separated from profane usage. I do not blow into these human bones to release the chants that they contain and that ancient rituals found in them, and I have no idea what rites to invent for them. They lie on a low table, the enigmatic center of my house now, around which friends and strangers gather, and we speak of their mystery.

In viewing them I am once again wrenched out of the whole

collection of tangible and usable things that fill my house, and I touch these bones lightly, as though my hand knows of itself that the nature of these sacred objects will not be uncovered by taking hold of them or exploring their contours. In the forms, my eyes and my fingers touch the substance: the bones now dark brown with age and incense, the silk threads bound in a band on them a third of the way down their length, and the fragile incense-browned, once pale blue gossamer wrappings. Holding these bone ritual horns in my hand, I feel myself falling, falling backward into the bodies of dying monks or of young virgins whose bones murmured mantras that would sound after they were dead. I cannot doubt that what I feel is a feeling a thousand years old, is what Buddhist monks or shamans dead generations ago felt when they held these bones with trembling hands and freed them from their silk wrappings.

But this certain, convinced feeling is divested of the least voice by historians of religion. Historical time, the time in practices, rituals, and conceptions that succeed one another, is progressive, linear or multilinear, and irreversible.

How many religions have gone extinct in the time of history! Plant and animal species are going extinct at the rate of 1,700 species a year, and every week, on average, someone dies who is the last speaker of one of the 6,800 human languages. Anthropologists rush to the remote jungles of the world to locate and record the cultures of peoples that are vanishing as the bulldozers and chain saws cut roads for the global technological society. Claude Lévi-Strauss wrote:

> Man himself appears as perhaps the most effective agent working toward the disintegration of the original order of things and hurrying on powerfully organized matter toward ever greater inertia, an inertia which will one day be final. From the time that he first began to breathe and eat, up to the invention of atomic and thermonuclear devices, by way of the discovery of fire—and except when he has been engaged

in self-reproduction—what else has man done except blithely break down billions of structures and reduce them to a state in which they are no longer capable of integration? No doubt he has built towns and cultivated the land; yet, on reflection, urbanization and agriculture are themselves instruments intended to create inertia, at a rate and in a proportion infinitely higher than the amount of organization they involve. As for the creations of the human mind, their significance only exists in relation to it, and they will merge into the general chaos as soon as the human mind has disappeared. Thus it is that civilization, taken as a whole, can be described as an extraordinarily complex mechanism, which we might be tempted to see as offering an opportunity of survival for the human world, if its function were not to produce what physicists call entropy, that is, inertia.[1]

In the historian's text, peoples and practices from far away and long ago return. They are recovered, reinstated, kept present in the historical representation. The historian's discourse establishes relations of significance between them. It positions past lives and events as the causes or conditions of the present. The historian's understanding retains from the past, not its forces and not its emotional forces, but its meanings. It envisions the future, at least history's own future, as an ever more complete representation of an ever more intelligible field and sequence of events. The historian's mind is the most comprehending mind. It reduces thousands of disparate, divergent organizations of forces and organisms of emotional force to the inert stillness of the historian's text.

At this late date of our culture we are spread-eagled on the vast text in which the imagery of our Judeo-Christian myths has been elaborated conceptually into theologies and in which the history of religions has recorded and conceptualized all the other religions. It is with the concepts of our system and the explanatory paradigms of our anthropology that scholars and intelligent travelers perceive, recognize, and conceptualize, for example, these ritual horns made from human bones. We then hold them as forensic scientists. We understand that we do not hold them as a monk or shaman once held them in a temple or cave in Mongolia generations ago. What our historically instructed mind can take hold of, in holding these bones, is only their meaning; we do not find in our hands the emotion and the force they imparted when they were functioning sacred objects. And the meaning we take hold of is a meaning we construct, out of the concepts in use in our anthropology and sociology of religions.

For the work of the anthropologist and historian is also a reduction of complex and diverse organizations to entropy, to inertia. "Each word exchanged, each line printed establish a communication between two interlocutors, leveling what until then was a divergence in information, that is, a greater organization," Lévi-Strauss says. "Instead of 'anthropology' we should name 'entropology,' the discipline that studies in its highest manifestations this process of disintegration."[2]

When Freud found that recovering and reinstating the memory of a traumatic event liberated the patient from a compulsive symptom, he understood that the symptom was a repetition, disguised or transposed, of an original traumatic event. In the symptom the fear, shock, or anxiety recurs. The memory that Freud recovered is also a repetition of the original trauma, but on another level, that of representation. To remember the traumatic event is to view it across a distance of time where it is pushed back in the lineup of all the events that have succeeded it, which takes from it its immediacy and immediate terror. The patient then repeats the real reactions to the trauma because he does not represent them, does not remember.

But does it not follow then that in order for the event to recur, to be repeated, it must not have been integrated into a representation, it must have been forgotten? If I relive a stretch of

time I have lived before, I do not also have now an accompanying memory of that prior stretch of life. The eternal recurrence
that Friedrich Nietzsche envisioned requires that one not now
live this life which, all in the same order and sequence, one has
lived before and also at the same time represent it to oneself as
a life one has lived before.

If for Freud's patients to recall a past event and to understand its meaning is to dissipate its force, does not the historian's mind strip the past, which it remembers and represents,
of its force? The historian confronts and scrutinizes the events
he represents; no longer advancing with the momentum of
their forces, she positions, connects, judges, evaluates, selects.
Historians of religion do not merely set aside any emotion with
which we approach this Mongolian ritual horn; in recording
its nature, context, function, and meanings on the plane of
representation, they dissipate the trembling emotion the hand
felt in contact with the substance of this incense-darkened
human bone. The representation prevents the recurrence of
that emotion.

Do not then events and initiatives from long ago and far
away have to be forgotten in order to recur with all their force?
Their force was the force of the hope and pride that surged
in them, the force of laughter and tears, blessings and cursings,
the force of love, trust, and faith. Hope and pride break with
the melancholy continuity of the past; they arise as forces
newly born, without a past. Love, trust, and faith arise with
the innocence, the candor, of forces disconnected from the
lessons of the past, the disabused prudence of the past. "There
could be no happiness, no cheerfulness, no hope, no pride, no
present, without forgetfulness," Nietzsche wrote.[3]

One is born with certain instincts, a certain sensibility,
certain tastes. It must have been Nietzsche's first and most enduring conviction, upon encountering Homer and Sophocles,
that he, and not the university scholars, understood them—
because he had the same instincts, the same sensibility, the

same taste. "It makes the most telling difference whether a thinker has a personal relationship to his problems and finds in them his destiny, his distress, and his greatest happiness, or an 'impersonal' one, meaning that he can do no better than to touch them and grasp them with the antennae of cold, curious thought."[4] This conviction, of understanding long-dead thinkers and artists because he found himself to be their blood brother, stamped what is most distinctive of Nietzsche's hermeneutics. Jesus was one of those blood brothers.

This conviction is no doubt the deepest source of the doctrine of eternal recurrence. A man born in the nineteenth century could be not of his time, could be not a modern man; his mentality could be not simply a singular compound of fragmentary systems of knowledge, incomplete stocks of information, and discontinuous paradigms drawn from the representations of nature and history that his culture has composed, along with disjoint fantasy fields. In a man lately born in the history of Europe there could recur the most ancient instincts, sensibilities, tastes, and dreams. Every pain and every joy and every thought and sigh and everything unutterably small or great in a life lived long ago could return with, for example, the birth of Friedrich Nietzsche. To the most comprehending mind of historians Nietzsche then opposes the most comprehensive soul "in which all things have their sweep and countersweep and ebb and flood," in which the instincts, sensibilities, and tastes from long ago and far away can recur, the soul then in whose time another time recurs.[5]

Will it be objected that Nietzsche speaks the language of his country and century, and that he also speaks with the interpretations embedded in the topics, categories, and classifications of that language? Will it be objected that anyone seeking to understand Homer or Sophocles has nothing but their texts, which the reader interprets in the categories and grammar of his own science and culture—texts where there are no facts, only interpretations and interpretations of interpretations? But

Nietzsche sees in the thought, practice, and institutions of a people deposited in texts the effects of the instincts, sensibility, and taste of that people. And these one understands inasmuch as they recur in oneself.[6]

For the historian, for the man of knowledge, the opinions, proofs, and refutations of Sophocles and the sages of the Rig Veda, Jesus, and Goethe—which are for Nietzsche symptoms of their instincts, sensibility, and taste—recur in himself in order to be transposed to the order of representation, where their ideal endurance puts an end to their real recurrence. For Nietzsche, when these atavistic instincts recur, they can maintain themselves in reality only by metamorphosing to that higher force that Nietzsche names nobility:

> What makes a person "noble"? . . . It involves the use of a rare and singular standard and almost a madness: the feeling of heat in things that feel cold to everybody else; the discovery of values for which no scales have been invented yet; offering sacrifices on altars that are dedicated to an unknown god; a courage without any desire for honors; a self-sufficiency that overflows and gives to men and things.[7]

> *A Kind of Atavism.*—I prefer to understand the rare human beings of an age as suddenly emerging late ghosts of past cultures and their powers—as atavisms of a people and its *mores.* . . . Now they seem strange, rare, extraordinary; and whoever feels these powers in himself must nurse, defend, honor, and cultivate them against another world that resists them, until he becomes either a great human being or a mad and eccentric one—or perishes early.

> Formerly, these same qualities were common and therefore considered *common*—not distinguished. Perhaps they were demanded or presupposed; in any case, it was impossible to become great through them, if only because they involved no danger of madness or solitude.

It is preeminently in the generations and castes that *conserve* a people that we encounter such recrudescences of old instincts.[8]

Against Rousseau's image of the noble savage, Nietzsche here presents the savage born too late, born in the midst of a civilized society; it is he who makes himself noble—or else perishes. The taste then, for things of long ago and far away, when one nurses it in oneself, defends it, honors and cultivates it, gives one that courage without any desire for honors, that self-sufficiency that overflows and gives to men and things.

How many gods have died! The gods of Olympus, the gods of Tenochtitlán, Wotan and Quetzalcoatl, Thor and Apollo and Agazu, the gods invoked in the stormy nights of Mongolia two thousand years ago. They died before the swords of the conquering people of other gods. Europeans were the first people to have put an end to the god of their own religion. Europe has put out its sun; it now revolves on a lonely planet in the darkness and emptiness of outer space:[9]

> Looking at nature as if it were proof of the goodness and governance of a god; interpreting history in honor of some divine reason, as a continual testimony of a moral world order and ultimate moral purposes; interpreting one's own experiences as pious people have long enough interpreted theirs, as if everything were providential, a hint, designed and ordained for the sake of the salvation of the soul—that is *all over* now, that has man's conscience *against* it, that is considered indecent and dishonest by every more refined conscience.[10]

Yet the religious impulses return. Particular instincts, sensibility, and taste can exist in the midst of a culture, a language, an economic and social context that no longer sustains them, that excludes them as the basis of participation in a community.

They do not exist in the linear or multilinear time of cultural and intellectual history. They exist in a time of nature, a time of periodic return.

When atavistic Zoroastrian instincts, sensibility, and taste recurred in someone born in post-Christian, scientific Germany, in Daniel Paul Schreber,[11] he felt powers in himself that he must nurse, defend, honor, and cultivate against a world that resists them, taking the risk of solitude or madness, until he became both a great human being and an eccentric and mad one—and perished early.

Christianity has been over for a very long time; there was only one Christian, Nietzsche declared, and he died on the cross. Yet there are millions, ever more millions now in Russia and in China who enlist in the ranks of Christian churches, Pauline churches, which have inverted the teaching that issued from the sensibility, the hypersensitivity of the redeemer-type, Jesus or the Buddha. There is then the task, which Nietzsche shouldered so forcefully, of showing that in the Christian institutions, ritual, and creed it is not the instincts, hyper-sensibility, and taste of Jesus that recurs, but instead the will to power, the hatreds, the monomania of the dysangelist Paul of Tarsus—and of Savonarola, Torquemada, Pius IX, Bob Jones, and Jerry Falwell.

When archaic religious instincts, sensibility, and taste recur, they can attach themselves to what are not religions at all. In this way they can mask even from themselves their religious character. They can take hold of the sphere of art, of politics, or even of the sciences, driving them with religious fervor and furor.[12]

And the religious instincts, sensitivity, and taste that recur may find themselves on the lookout for quite new and separate domains to invest. Could then archaic religious instincts, sensitivity, and taste return to invest regions from which all gods have vanished?[13]

—And how many new gods are still possible! As for myself, in whom the religious, that is to say god-forming, instinct occasionally becomes active at impossible times—how differently, how variously the divine has revealed itself to me each time! So many strange things have passed before me in those timeless moments that fall into one's life as if from the moon, when one no longer has any idea how old one is or how young one will yet be—[14]

Here, in this late text, Nietzsche equates the religious instinct with the god-forming instinct. But earlier Nietzsche had understood that the god-forming instinct is but one peculiar avatar of the religious instinct:

One still believes . . . in a gradual evolution of *representations of gods* from clumsy stones and blocks of wood up to complete humanization: and yet the fact of the matter is that, *so long as* the divinity was introduced into trees, pieces of wood, stones, animals, and felt to reside there, one shrank from a humanization of their form as from an act of godlessness.[15]

Should we then regret the extinction of the god-forming compulsion? "There is not enough love and goodness in the world for us to be permitted to give any of it away to imaginary things."[16] Should we not instead reserve our love for ancient bones and for blocks of stone?

Lalibela

*T*HE PLACE ONCE CALLED ROHA and now called Lalibela
is in one of the most inaccessible heights in the Ethiopian
mountains. Until 1995, to get there you had to ride eight days
on a mule from Addis Ababa; now there is a road and you need
two days by Jeep or Land Cruiser. You are there, you are walking over the bare rock flank of a mountain, and suddenly you
find yourself on the edge of a deep pit in which is lying a huge
Greek cross cut in the rock. After a moment you realize that
this rock cross lying just below the level of your feet is the roof
of a stone building. You are looking down on the Beta Giorgis,
the church of Saint George, carved and hollowed out of solid
rock. There is no plaza cut away to view it; to descend to the
church you go down a narrow winding passage opened at some
distance and tunneling to the bottom of the pit. The church
stands on a plinth with a flight of stairs cut to the entrance.
The rock is pinkish red in color, splashed with yellow lichens.
There are only some ten feet from the church to the side walls
of the pit; in the walls you see tunnels bored to what are the
cells of hermit priests. Some of these priests are reading prayers;
if one notices you he greets you with folded hands and a bow.
One tunnel leads through the mountain to a place where,
nearby on another level, you come upon another church standing
in its square pit. Rising and descending through tunnels, you
eventually come upon thirteen churches carved and hollowed

out in the rock of the mountain, some of them freestanding, their base continuous with the mountain like the Giorgis, others with one or more walls that are one with the mountain. According to archaeologists Ewald Hein and Brigitte Kleidt,

> It is quite simply not known who had the churches . . . built, when and in what order they were hewn from the living rock . . . , whether there was a master builder by the name of Sidi Maskal and where he came from, whether Copts fleeing from Egypt, where they were subject to persecution in the 12th/13th centuries under the Mamelukes, brought their skills with them and had a decisive influence, or were just workers among others. Even the method of working is unknown; it is only possible to draw conclusions on how it might have been from technical needs.
>
> What understanding of the world led to the monolithic churches of Lalibela remains obscure. . . . The majority are in keeping with Orthodox style, with a basilical floor plan, a dome above the sanctuary, three doors at the west end necessary for the rites and orientation towards the east.
>
> And it remains quite uncertain why in fact these churches were hewn. . . . Was the custom of the Agaw to celebrate rites in caves transferred into a new dimension of self-portrayal? Were they seeking—understandably enough after the almost complete destruction of Axumite civilisation in the wars of the 10th century—indestructibility? But rock-hewn churches, such as Cherkos Wukro or Abreha Atsbeha, were not, it is true, destroyed, but irreparably damaged. . . . Did they want to copy those in the capital Axum out of political calculations while at the same time surpassing them with creations magically entrusted to the bowels of the Earth? Were they even taking up the myth of the foundation of Ethiopia—the taking of the Ark of the Covenant, the creation of a new Jerusalem? The omnipresent "sacral geography" in Lalibela speaks in favour of this thesis. Shrines bear names such as

Golgotha, Debre Sina or Bethlehem, mountains and rivers
are called Tabor and Jordan. Here too it may be a retrospec-
tive attempt by the new rulers to make the Lalibela myth
serve their purposes.[1]

Hein and Kleidt speak of indestructibility, but the visitor to
Ethiopia today sees destructibility everywhere; in the populations, ravaged this year again by famine; in the war, civil war
since the deposition of Haile Selassie and war with Eritrea;
and in continual skirmishes with Sudan and Somalia. The
United Nations places Ethiopia 171st on its list of 174 countries
graded according to development; only Sierra Leone, Chad,
and Niger are worse off. The deforestation has been devastating in the last decades; now only 3 percent forest cover remains,
and millions of tons of soil are lost each year to erosion. Some
of the rock churches of Lalibela have been covered with scaf-
folding and tin roofs, and they are visibly crumbling.

The millions of pilgrims who trek to Lalibela on high feast
days surely bear witness to the persistence of Christianity in
Ethiopia, which, with the conversion of King Ezana in 330,
became the first Christian country. It's a peculiarly African
Christianity, Coptic, Monophysite in theology, and in it an
archaic pre-Talmudic Judaism returns. The altars of Ethiopia
do not contain, as in Europe, fragments of the true cross, but
instead copies of the *tabot,* the Ark of the Covenant, which,
according to Ethiopians, was spirited out of the Temple of
Jerusalem by Menelik I, son of Solomon and the Queen of Sheba.

Yet how much is lost here of the rock-hewn churches of
Lalibela—their origins, their designers, their dates, the political and economic organization of the society that carved them,
the theological conceptions in which they made sense. I wandered from tunnel to tunnel, and the churches I saw became
more inconceivable. I could not imagine, somewhere around
1250, a ruler or high priest gathering thousands of people here,
high on the summit of these mountains, and infecting them

with some dream of his, to chisel thirteen churches, one next to another, out of the barren rock flank of this mountain fastness. It is also inconceivable that anything like this could ever again be wrought on our planet. Today carving these thirteen churches, if anyone could assemble the funds to do it, would be done in a year with power machines.

Once there, however, you want to stay on for weeks, for months. You feel the separateness of the churches of Lalibela from the Monophysite theologies that conceptualized and programmed them, from the feudal society that drafted thousands of men to chisel them out, from the history in which they took form and which sank away from them into oblivion, and their separateness too from all the traffic of our moment of history. Wandering in and out of these churches you feel the instincts of their carvers, you find resurging in yourself an instinct for the depths of rock, a sensibility for the stillness, the silence, the inexpressibility. You find resurging in yourself an instinct to live here, simultaneously burrowed into the depths of rock and standing on top of the Ethiopian mountains, seeing as eagles see. Wherever you wander from now on, across Ethiopia, across Africa, across oceans and continents, there will be something in you that has become, ineradicably, a pilgrim, who, God willing, will return to Lalibela.

From his cell carved in the rock walls beside a church, a hermit greets you like a brother.

Vodou

*T*HERE IS A CONSIDERABLE, and ancient, literature that depicts the explosive movement in ecstasy as an ascent to the good. The concept of good designates plenitude, achievement, a final state, an enduring state. A disequilibrium, a breach in the good that makes it pass, is a flaw in the good. God is the good substantized. But we have ceased to trust the good, as we no longer trust beauty, truth, or virtue.

Our culture no longer knows any sacred places, such as those where Javanese and Tibetans went to undergo inward transfiguration. The transport and awe that the Orphics and the Mongolians and the Quichol Indians sought in the monstrous and terrifying forms of their religious ecstasies—these have modern Westerners sought in high art. Now film studios produce electronic mirages more marvelous than those of the old masters. Instead of being thrown into trance before unknown powers, we are entertained by their laser-beam epiphanies; our minds understand the devices and tricks that the electronic engineers have used.

Two centuries of militant positivism combated as superstition the beliefs of prescientific Europe. Having discredited as legends the creeds of the Aztecs, the Yoruba, and the Easter Islanders, Westerners destroyed their own religion with scientific skepticism. Science is now discarding and replacing its cosmological and biological theories too rapidly for anyone to take the current representation of human nature, animal nature, and chemical and electromagnetic nature as true.

Mindful of the two wars in which Western countries plunged the world, of the global plunder they now pursue, mouthpieces of Western ideologies no longer give lessons of virtue. Talk of the good life only evokes images of sybaritic self-indulgence.

Ecstasy had its uses. Sacrifices of resources and lives, as well as feasting and orgy, were found to be expenditures useful for achieving victory in war. Sacrificing oneself was seen as a means to achieve equality and justice for the community on earth. Sacrifice was also taken to be a means to achieve personal salvation in another life. Throughout history, reasons were developed for an individual to head for extreme states, to stake his very life on them. These reasons have fallen away. Deprived of faith in another life, stripped of hope even for an egalitarian and just community worth dying for, we have no motives for seeking ecstatic states of abnegation.

The obscure longing for the spiritual that still stirs among us today is not a search for something achieved and final, some plenary substance. Whatever is substantial and stable appears to us to have no sacred reality. We understand it to be correlative with the manipulative, appropriating, accumulative lusts of work, reason, and technology. The contemporary spirit looks up to what can be encountered only by chance, not by method and calculation. In moments of rupture, when fissures appear in the chains of discontinuous substances that reason and technology line up in the world of work, the sacred breaks through, fleeing before it can be appropriated. We then have not ceased to know and to believe in ecstasy—but in the form of eruptions of joy before these fleeting moments.

The longing for ecstasy, wherever it has been elaborated in texts and in institutional practices, has most often involved asceticism. For us it seems implausible that the release of the soul to travel vast distances could occur in the anesthetized sensibility and constrained sensuality of a debilitated body. Yet it also seems true that ecstasy surges from the lower depths of the psyche, the body, and society. Those who find ecstasy do so not by visiting the shrines of civilization but by trudging the swamps of human destitution and misery. Our literature of ecstasy recounts dark nights of the soul and encounters with mystics in slums and in refugee camps of genocidal wars.

There is a mystic or masochistic tradition in Christianity that reverses the forces of the world and finds in the beggars and street orphans a force stronger than that of civil society and economy, a supernatural force. Mohandas Gandhi had traversed the length and breadth of India in third-class railway cars. He saw the force of those who rule; he also saw the force of those who suffer, who have or find the force to endure the worst that nature and institutional cruelty can lay on lives. He came to see in the mobs of beggars around the train stations the force that would liberate India.

The forms of ecstasy that survive among us are subject to every kind of rational mistrust. Ecstasy has been cut free from its ancient bonds with practical asceticism and intellectual idealism, but it fails to find a place in our psychological, sociological, and political rationality.

Since ecstasy is communication with what is sacred, remote from ourselves, it is communication with others, too. There is no such thing as a private ecstasy. Since ecstasy is a breaking out of solitude, out of the self, since it is a communication, it appears as an event in history. Though it breaks with political methods and institutions, it has a political impact. Afterward one will judge it from its social consequences. Did the leader who opened the floodgates of ecstatic emotions manipulate and use the people? Did he deceive them, betray them? Or, simply, did the moment of ecstasy delude the people into thinking that something was possible when all that was possible was a return of oppression in another guise? Our sociological and political rationality can justify only democracy where political decisions are reached through rational programs tested and reappraised by rational debate. After two thousand years of ecstasies before the crucifixion of Jesus, we are suspicious of alleged mystics on the margins of well-ordered society. We read Don Juan and remember Rasputin. Are not the forces of our ecstasies those of cruel lusts that dare not speak their name?

Every kind of ecstatic literature identifies the ecstatic joy with loss of self. Is there not inevitably something like a collapse of the ideals of self-affirmation, courage, and bodily integrity? Is there not a cruelty toward oneself in all ecstatic loss of self? What unrecognized glands and nerves connect the ecstatic loss of self with pathological masochism?

The university. The world of work and reason. For me it had been a full day. Two classes to teach. Then an hour in the office, talking noncommittally with some students who want to get a better grade. Then a departmental colloquium meeting. The speaker read a paper legitimated with citations of canonical authors and written in the philosophical idiom currently fashionable in Europe, weighted with Greek and German words. During the reading, one tries to think up a sophisticated question to put to the speaker when he finishes. Afterward there was dinner with the speaker and other faculty members. The conversation turned on who got tenure, who moved to a better university. Then we moved on to the reception for the speaker, hosted by a senior professor in his big bland house. At such gatherings one congratulates a colleague about a paper he tells you he has recently published; one asks a student about her dissertation topic. One gets some well-mannered flatteries in return. I kept an eye out for a couple who had to leave early to relieve the babysitter, and, inventing some early morning commitment, I left, too.

I poured myself a strong drink to put an end to a day spent with duties. I lay on my bed, paging through the *New York*

Times. Then a small item caught my eyes: the airport at Port-au-Prince was opened today. Exiled President Aristide was to return in two days. Drunk already, I flopped across the bed to the phone, rang the airline. I was able to get a seat for the ten o'clock flight the next morning. At midnight a friend called; I told him that in an hour I was driving to New York to catch a plane for Port-au-Prince. In a half hour he was downstairs, with toothbrush and razor in a paper bag.

Haitians had waged the second revolution against a European colonial power in the hemisphere, the first successful slave revolt in history. Even Thomas Jefferson took alarm at the spectacle of a slave population rising up and massacring their masters; the United States did not recognize independent Haiti until after the American Civil War. Black, Creole-speaking Haiti occupies but a third of the island of Hispaniola (the other side is the Dominican Republic, predominantly white and Spanish-speaking) and is hopelessly overpopulated. The rocky mountainous terrain has been denuded of its trees, and the sea below is brown with tons of soil oozing down with every rain. Whatever wealth there is is in the hands of a tiny oligarchy of mulattoes who affect French language and culture. As soon as it had acquired independence, the new nation had fallen into the hands of a succession of bloodthirsty caudillos.

During the latter years of the reign of Baby Doc Duvalier, in a church in Port-au-Prince a little priest was filling his sermons with images of slavery. His name was Jean-Bertrand Aristide. His church was bombed by the *Tontons Makout.* After the death of Duvalier, foreign powers with economic or strategic interests in Haiti arranged for elections. Aristide got elected president. Virtually the only regular wage labor in Haiti was in the three hundred U.S. assembly plants; Sears exported sixty-seven million dollars' worth of assembled textiles in one year, paying its Haitian workers eleven cents an hour, though the Haitian legal minimum wage was twenty-five cents an hour. President Aristide introduced legislation increasing it to thirty-seven cents an hour. The Bush administration worked to destabilize the Aristide regime, and the CIA armed the FRAPH death squads.[1] The U.S. press carried reports that Aristide was mentally unstable; there were mentions of breakdowns, treatments. Overthrown by Colonel Raoul Cédras, Aristide fled to the United States, taking lodging in Harlem. He spent his evenings playing his guitar. Thousands of Haitians began fleeing in rafts, some of which made it to Florida. President Clinton had ordered them returned to Haiti, but the black caucus in Congress began to put pressure on the president to do something. The Clinton administration imposed an embargo, which forced the assembly plants for Sears and other U.S. companies in Haiti to close. In Congress, Senator Bob Dole argued that Haiti is of no strategic importance to the United States and stated simply: Haiti is not worth one American life. But that did not stem the flotilla of rafts, many of which were lost at sea.

Eventually Clinton decided to send in the marines. For Haiti is of strategic interest to the United States: Hispaniola is the sister island to Cuba. Across the border, in the Dominican Republic, dictator Trujillo's last prime minister, the now-blind Edouardo Joacquín Balaguer, was recently fraudulently re-elected president for the seventh time. The United States now prepared for his demise, the U.S. ambassador pressuring him to agree to a new election in two years. So it was time to establish a U.S. Marine presence in Haiti. Then the United States would be prepared for the inevitable death of Fidel Castro and his regime.

We saw marines everywhere; any other white people turned out to be journalists. I regretted not thinking to bring white shorts, a flowered sports shirt, and straw hat. Having learned that journalists got their passes for the Presidential Palace from the U.S. Marine office near the port, we went first thing in the morning. When I handed over my press card the officer said,

"I don't know this one; what agency are you with?" Whoops—
I had never really looked at what it said when I bought it some
years earlier from an elevator operator in Bangkok. But the
officer satisfied himself by reading the card; it did not occur to
him that any foreigners other than journalists were there. My
friend identified himself as my photographer, and when the
officer turned around to answer the phone, my friend slipped
a copy of the pass form from his desk; when we were out of the
building he filled it in.

The white building of the Presidential Palace was surrounded by three rings of marines in full combat gear. Each
officer that passed us on gave us more credibility. Finally we
were inside, in the garden before the palace gleaming under
the sun in its new coat of white paint.

We had been told that Aristide would arrive at ten o'clock.
Since the worst-case scenario for the United States was for
Aristide to be shot by a sniper upon arrival, there was to be
no motorcade; he was to be flown by U.S. military helicopter
directly from the airport to the Presidential Palace. All around
the garden, pressing against the iron rods of the high fence,
were thousands of Haitians, most of whom had spent the night
there. Marines in helmets and flak jackets and holding auto-
matic rifles faced them from inside the fence. On the roofs
of the buildings surrounding the square we could see armed
marines scanning the crowd with binoculars.

Hours passed. On one side of the palace under the trees were
some cages of white doves, watched over by marines holding
machine guns. The sun blazed overhead; the air was boiling.
Then suddenly a violent windstorm twisted the great mango
trees to the left of the palace and a big military helicopter was
there, hovering, descending to the ground. It had flown in
low, the palace had hidden its coming from us. We raced over
to it; the crowd outside the fence cried out and then hushed.
Under its clattering blades five men descended and strode quickly to the building between rows of crouching marines turned

in all directions with their machine guns. The blades of the
helicopter did not stop; as soon as the men who descended had
cleared them the helicopter immediately rose, and almost at
once another tornado battered the trees: a second helicopter
was there. As soon as the men who descended from it were
rushed to the palace, this helicopter too roared off, as a third
swung into its place. Still no Aristide. But we began recognizing some people: Jesse Jackson, John Kennedy Jr., Warren
Christopher. They soon appeared on the balcony over the
palace entrance, standing with members of Aristide's government, no doubt, and U.S. high officials. And then another
helicopter, and a small black man descended, in a dark blue
suit with a wide sash crossing his chest: Aristide. He turned
to the crowd and hailed them as the marines rushed him into
the palace. But rushing toward him from all sides like a tidal
wave was the roar of the crowd. The ground trembled under
its onrush. It drowned the racket of the helicopter, it surged
up into the sky. My heart was pounding, my chest heaving.
I was gasping for air in panic; my body was being swept away
in the thunder breaking forth from the earth. The sky was the
only space great enough for this tidal wave of joy, the sky that
unites those who breathe under its shelter, that unites us even
with beings to come.

Suddenly a force had surged up from a destitute, un-
employed, unskilled, uneducated crowd, a crowd without
a future, without hope, with nothing to give to their children
or to humanity or to me. It was a force as strong as the might
of the marines outfitted in battle gear, of the warships an-
chored offshore, of the fighter planes and bombers poised to
blacken the sky. The force of life, of naked life; no, the force
of their destitution and despair.

Aristide disappeared into the building. Some minutes later
he appeared at the dais set up on the steps of the palace to
address the crowd. He was shielded from snipers' bullets but
also from the crowd by the bulletproof glass cage. He called

for peace and reconciliation. He appealed to the crowd not to take vengeance on the *toutons macoutes,* their torturers. He was reciting the piece the U.S. State Department had prepared for him. The white doves that had been released had taken shelter from the sun on the upper windows.

The men who pressed against the iron grill fence of the garden no longer felt their hunger under the burning skies, the old women no longer felt their cramps, the young women no longer felt their fatigue as they held their infants. A meteoric object pulled open the prison gates of consciousness upon the distances, the depths, and the heights. This object could be a typhoon sudden and devastating, a bolt of lightning in the mid-day sky, or a frail little man. The ecstatic object is not an object of observation. It is not a focal point of a significant field where the whole context, made of meaningful relations, sets forth a figure in relief. It is not the goal of a practical layout; it is outside the means, the relay points, of initiatives and enterprises. The Haitians had left the field of the practicable the previous night when they left their homes to come here. But the ecstatic object is also not some condensed image or symbol of perfection, of peace, of utopia, of the divine. Arbitrary, even derisory, it unleashes the anonymous tornado of joy rising to the universal sky.

The state of ecstasy then is not any kind of project. It is even indifferent to the effects that may result from it. It is remote from all morality—unless it be the morality of the Bhagavad Gita.

Viewed from the outside, from the point of view of political and social history, the ecstasy of the crowd before the Presidential Palace is dangerous to the social order, dangerous thus to themselves. But every ecstasy can only appear as fraught with danger.

"Ecstasy explains nothing, illuminates nothing, and justifies nothing," Georges Bataille wrote. "It is nothing more than a flower, necessarily as incomplete, as perishable as a flower. . . .

Take then a flower and look at it until your gaze accords with it such that it explains, illuminates, and justifies by being incomplete, by being perishable."[2] Life is most intensely, profoundly alive when it hurls itself toward the unknown in order to become ignorant, stupefied, dazzled. When all their forces are released, humans seek out the greatest dangers. Life is essentially extravagant; life is an extravagance in the interlockings and gearings of the world.

The ecstatic reception for Aristide was to be without consequence. The U.S. authorities had gotten Aristide to agree to new elections within a year. He would be constitutionally ineligible for a second successive term. At year's end then he left the Presidential Palace, abandoned his priesthood, married, and moved into a mansion with a swimming pool surrounded by armed guards. The next time the elections came around, his followers rigged them such that there was no chance he would not be elected and the full Parliament with him. But the elections were not recognized internationally. International aid was withheld, leaving the economy and the lot of the people more hopeless than before.

If Haiti is not worth one American life, there was also nothing there for me. I could in no way contribute to Haitian economy or society. There was nothing I could bring back from the garden of the Presidential Palace—no thoughts, no insights, no knowledge usable elsewhere. I was not an outsider, inside the garden, observing the crowd. I was lost in them, in the groundswell of their joy. I had stolen five days from my teaching duties at the university. I would return to my routines there.

Breakout

*H*ILARY HAD TAKEN ME WITH HER to help her decide
about purchasing a house in a small town on the edge of
greater London. The house was also small and had the prim
conventional shape of so many houses in so many English
towns. The prior owners could say little to justify the asking
price, and Hilary had to calculate and recalculate her finances
to see if she could afford it. To persuade her, the owners kept
us outside most of the time, in the quite large yard. They had
planted the front with rare roses and flowering quinces; in the
walled rear garden flagstone paths led between raised beds to
two gazebos whose trellises were covered with clematis vines.
The owners led us down the paths, identifying on either side
of the paths azaleas, Asiatic boxwoods, oakleaf hydrangeas,
buddleias, tree peonies, Japanese iris, lungworts, Carpathian
bellflowers, foxgloves, Oriental lilies. The beds were also
planted with thousands of tulips, daffodils, jonquils, Siberian
squills, now dormant but which, the owners told us, spread
blazes of color from earliest spring. We were dumbfounded by
the botanical erudition and unremitting industriousness of the
owners, which set them apart in this mediocre town where we
had imagined only drab and conventional lives.

The following spring I was in England again, and on a warm
late afternoon went to find Hilary. I had to check the house
number to be sure I had found the right house: the roses and

quinces were gone; the front yard was nothing but bare ground. No one answered the bell; I went around to the back and found Hilary, disheveled and joyous, driving her spade into the clumps of plants and overturning them. She embraced me with mucky arms and pulled me down on the soft lumps of overturned ground. We studied the whitish roots that twisted around one another in delirious masses and dug our fingers into the dirt to pull out rhizomes and bulbs, fat and white as tumors. We began tossing them at one another and, when darkness descended, pulled off our clothes and tossed them at one another and embraced on the warm earth. The next morning I asked Hilary what she was going to plant now, and she laughed: "Nothing!"

It was a year later that I went to spend a week with her again. The house was now surrounded with prairie. Wild grasses, clovers, and all kinds of plant stems branching into tiny flowers and furry seedpods were knee-high. "They came by themselves," she said, "flown in with the wind." The bare earth surface I had last seen was now everywhere throbbing with their frenetic compulsion to rise upward to the sun. Already here and there tree seedlings were pushing up and taking off. Hilary had restored the flagstone walls of the raised beds, and the paths were scrupulously swept clean. "I do that because," she said, "the neighbors complained that I had let the garden go to weeds and sent an official over from the Council. I told him I was a botanist and had planted each of the species individually for research purposes. He didn't look too convinced, but he wrote his report and hasn't come back." We lay in the warm late-afternoon sun and inspected at random the pale little flowers over our heads. I was back in my childhood on the farm, where I used to disappear for hours in the densely overgrown gullies and knew my first orgasms.

Once upon a time apes descended from the trees, advanced into the savanna, and stood upright. Though geographers refer to savannas, prairies, tundras, and steppes as grasslands, typically but 20 percent of the plants there are grasses; there is also a great variety of legumes and composites, algae, mosses, and orchids. Wood and tree leaves are mostly cellulose and lignin, but the grassland plants are high in pectin and protein, available in the whole tissue of the plants. Flowering plants produce seeds, embryos with concentrated stores of nutrients. Grasslands support a great diversity of animal life: insects that coevolved with flowering plants; birds that live on insects and on seeds, which they also scatter and plant; small and large mammals—hoofed herbivores and big carnivores and primates. The human apes did not give up contact with the trees, which they sought for shade and rest and which they climbed for safety and for the view.

When our moralists speak of living according to nature and respecting nature and our own nature, it is the spectacle of flourishing fields and forests, rising upright from the earth to the sun, that they invoke. It is fields and forests that the ancient Stoics, Emerson and Thoreau, Nietzsche and Hegel, the evolutionists with their tree or multistemmed bush of evolution and the ecologists of today see as the natural landscape of human rectitude and justice. Our subspecies of primate, standing erect, respects the upright, equivalent for us to dignity; esteems rectitude, for us equivalent to righteousness; values the elevated and praises eyes turned to the skies and the heavens, for us equivalent to the decent, the noble, the ideal, the sacred.

The sequoias, great upright poles rising two hundred and fifty feet into the sky with only the sparsest of branches, are celebrated as the most noble of trees. The endurance of those trees that have seen so many peoples and societies and regimes come and go in the course of the twenty-five hundred years they've lived materializes fortitude and steadfastness for us. We tolerate, with bad conscience, the commercialization of our artists, our women, even our churches, but shrink back from cutting down the giant sequoias for timber. As long as they stand tall there is still something noble and just in America.

The branches and the twigs of the linden trees and great elms presiding over the main streets of our towns give us the vision of an architectural order, an ordered distribution of each part in its own place, post, and function—a compelling everyday vision of justice and harmony. Each in its place, the individual leafy stems exhibit purpose and dignity. When we come upon cities without trees we feel we have come upon zones of moral collapse.

But other emotions also emerge in fields and forests. Below the trunks and stems of fields and forests rising to the sun, roots descend and wind and knot and wallow like worms in the wet earth, lured by rank decomposition. They, however, must not be seen. Roots turned up in the air and sun die, and the whole plant dies with them; floods and storms that uproot the fields and the forests are disasters. The sequoias are not the oldest monuments in nature; in Africa and Australia there are baobab trees that are also twenty-five hundred years old. They have thick squat trunks, and then a brushy tangle of branches that look like the roots of trees uprooted by storms, and sparse leaves on those branches. They struck European traders and explorers as the very image of what is inverted, perverted, in darkest Africa. Our visceral sense of the base, the low, the mean, the vile in certain behaviors, attitudes, and inclinations designates their affinity with the dark and dank earth, with rot and decay.[1]

Some roots are particularly indecent. The mandrake root, short, thick, white, and bulbous, often branching into two at the bottom and often branching twice, presents an obscene image of a naked human body, headless and without muscle delineation. Carrots look too much like human penises, turnips like swollen testicles. These images give us the sense that there are base roots in our bodies—our clitorises, our penises, our naked fingers and toes pushing in disordered directions when our bodies have let go of their upright posture and uprightness in the night. To expose in the air and sunlight these dissolute bodies, these roots pushing into sweat and darkness, would be a moral disaster.[2] Yet intense emotions course tumultuously in these base organs of our bodies and into all subterranean nature.

Storms of orgasm overturn our bodies. Our posture, which holds our body upright and directed upon tasks, collapses, no longer integrating our limbs and sense organs, each in its own place, post, and function. Our eyes no longer scan the environment for the right path; our gaze drifts. Our hands and legs roll about without purpose or dignity. Our fingers fondle the mounds and orifices of another's body with aimless, repetitious movements, not exploring, not learning anything. The sighs and moans of another pulse through the nervous networks of our body; spasms of pleasure and torment in another's body shudder across our cheeks, belly, thighs. Our excitements expire in sweat and genital secretions and releases of hot moist breath over our beds damp as springtime earth. In the anxiety and exhilaration of orgasm, convulsion of what the ancients called our vegetative soul, we sink into the living depth of our nature and into the depths of vegetative nature.

In the south of Peru stands the white colonial city of Arequipa, its mansions, Mudejar churches, and monasteries made of carved blocks of white volcanic tufa. From there we took a four-and-a-half-hour truck ride on the dirt road around the volcanoes Misti, Chiacoan, and Pichi-Pichi. The terrain is all volcanic tufa, swirls of white crust as if poured out of a bowl, and so arid it is almost completely devoid of vegetation.

At length we reached the brink of a great fault in the continental tectonic plate: the Colca Canyon. Far below, a meandering river has dug it to depths deeper than any other canyon on the planet. A path descends the flank of the canyon. Here and there at the bottom of the canyon there are some Indian hamlets. These people were passed over by the Inca Empire and are too alien and too poor to be enlisted in the Peruvian state today. I was able to find lodging for the night. The full moon shone in crystal splendor; seeing it between the narrow walls of the canyon was like looking at it through a tube. On the upper edges of the canyon its light poured over the glaciers. I walked down the lanes, sensing the discreet but trusting proximity of the dark forms of strangers. I ended up in a room where four young men were playing a llama-hide drum, reed pipes, and two stringed gourds. The music had wild rhythms that pulled me up from my seat to dance and tragic melodies that tore at the heart. A young man knew just enough Spanish words to propose guiding me in the morning. He said his name was Santiago.

We set out at four o'clock. The natural terrain, from the glaciers down sheer bare rock and then to the slopes created by erosion and down into the deep gorge cut by the river, was a display of ever different cuts, different colors of cliffs, rocks, and clay. Over generations, the people had carved the canyon with the subtle eyes and patience of diamond-cutters; the flanks of the canyon from the river up hundreds of feet were faceted with stone-walled terraces. The terraces were growing quinoa, potatoes, and many species of high-altitude corn that were irrigated by the melting glaciers and the springs and cascades that release the ground water.

On the terraces and in the hamlets below, the women wore long multicolored bouffant skirts and broad-rimmed hats; as the canyon turned around mountains I noticed that the hat style differed in different settlements. Later back in Arequipa I read in a book on the native populations of Peru that two different populations settled the canyon, revering two different sacred *Apus,* mountains. They reflected the forms of their respective sacred mountains on their own heads, placing molds on their infants' skulls so that, in one people, their skulls would be cylindrical and in the other, flat on top. When the missionaries collected the people into fortified villages called *reducciones,* they forbade skull-molding of children and imposed Spanish dress. The one group then devised high and cylindrical hats, the other high, flat-topped hats.

On both sides the mountains above were glacier-covered, but volcano Mount Sabancaya was gushing out dense clouds of smoke. At a place called Maca, Santiago indicated that earthquakes had shaken down a village two years ago and now the quakes were starting up again at the same spot. We went down to look at a big crack; the local people told Santiago, and he conveyed to me by pointing to hours back on my watch, that it had just opened up the prior night. Our slow and wearing ascent up the canyon, the grit crumbling under our shoes, measured the time of our effort and of our life against the geological epochs of the planet's crust and rock layers. The scale of geological time diminishes us and destines any footprints we leave here, indeed any works we build in our lifetime, to erosion and mineral decomposition.

We trekked to the top of the terracing and, chewing coca leaves, climbed ever higher; finally we reached Condor's Cross, where the canyon is deepest.[3] It is also very narrow, a knife-cut through twelve thousand feet of rock, at the bottom of which, like a crinkle of mercury, we saw the river. All around, the glaciers of the Andes began to blaze with the rising sun. Loftiest is the volcano Mount Mismi, whose melting glacier is the source of the Amazon. The sulfurous fumes of the Sabancaya volcano we passed hours ago in the dark are billowing in the sky. We settled on a boulder in this uninhabitable mountainscape. No human enterprise could take hold here; I could form no project here, not even an exploratory hike. Even if I had any shreds of vocabulary of his language or he of mine, I would not have anything to say to my Indian companion, not even any question to ask him. The discursive movements of the mind, staking out paths, laying out positions and counterpositions, were silenced. As soon as the sun emerged over the peaks of the Andes, it turned the cloudless sky magnesium-white. Its radiation spread over our faces and hands like warmth, although the thin air my heaving lungs were pumping in was cold.

After a long time spent motionless, I become aware that the sun is now high in the sky. And then, well before seeing it, we are aware of the condor, like a silent drumroll in the skies over the glaciers. Our eyes are pulled to a speck taking form in the empty radiance, imperceptibly becoming bigger, becoming a great bird never once flapping or even shifting its wings, gliding down from a great height and then into the canyon, descending to eye level in front of us before gradually descending deeper and becoming lost to sight. It is the first condor I have seen, with its fifteen-foot wingspan the largest flying bird on the planet; this one is brown, a young female. She is perhaps surveying the desolate cliffs and avalanches for carrion; perhaps she has already fed and is continuing her daylong life in the heights. And then—an hour, two hours later?—there are two: again we know they are there well before they are visible. They are close to one another, circling companionably in the airless heights. When they are overhead, I try to gauge their height, judging that they are above us halfway again the depth of the canyon—that is, some eighteen thousand feet. I, who could hardly climb much higher than our present thirteen thousand feet, feel my eyes, my craving, my fascination plunging to their almost immaterial realm, falling up into the region of death. We are nothing but a vision, a longing, a euphoric outflow of life hanging on to the flight of the condors. Their flight comes from a past without memory and soars into a future without anticipation. We are cut loose, unanchored, without guy wires, drifting in the void of the sky. We feel nothing but the thin icy air, see nothing but the summits and ice cliffs of the Andes and the granite walls of the canyon below. We are alive for nothing but for their bodies and their flight.

Climbing the rocky coves and promontories of Sydney Harbor hoping to catch sight of whales, mocked by the swift slippery seals, one gets tired. One hundred seventy pounds of mostly salty brine in an unshapely sack of skin—one's legs fold and strain to hoist this weight; the joints ache. How one can understand the dolphins and whales, mammals who evolved on land but long ago returned to the ocean! Still, movement on Earth's surface is not simply a blunder on the part of evolution, as the cases of serpents and cheetahs show. And after all, one can also return to the ocean with the whales and seals, strapping on an air tank and fins.

At closing time, I went back to the Manley Oceanarium. The staff had given me leave to enter the shark tank after hours with scuba gear. If walking across a continent's surface carrying my body weight on jointed legs was awkward enough, doddering across the basement of the Oceanarium with buoyancy compensator, air tank, regulator and gauges, face mask, weight belts, and flippered feet was ludicrous. But once inside the tank, having achieved buoyancy, I could slide through the water with my rubber fins. I gaped in wonder at how different the light and colors of the water looked compared with the view from the visitors' tunnel. Of course it is still diving in an artificial reef. But the Oceanarium is so big (the tank holds 4.6 million liters; the staff said they do not know how many animals are in there—thousands) that the behavior of the animals is not different from the behavior of creatures in the ocean. And in a lifetime of diving the oceans, how often could one get that close to great sharks! I was told to avoid letting them bump into me and not to touch them, for sharks, like all fish, have a slime coating on their skin that protects them from bacterial infections and that my touch could break. For an hour I watched huge sharks passing inches from my eyes and great rays folding their bodies over my head.

It is the cartilage, not bones, they have that gives them their extraordinary suppleness of movement. Their sleek bodies are as hydrodynamic as our bodies holding themselves up off the ground are unaerodynamic. The rays are classified by science as belonging to the same family, but their movement is totally different from that of sharks; they are disks that shimmer and glide. Our bodies walk in a succession of falls stopped by a lurching of bones; their whole bodies ripple musically. Their movement is disinterested; movement is the nature of their life. Cold-blooded animals have to eat much less than do warm-blooded ones. Sharks go for weeks, even a whole winter, without eating at all. In the Oceanarium, it is a real job to get them to eat a fish to please the viewing tourists. They just keep cruising by. Liz has to stuff a fish into their jaws, and most of the time they refuse to bite down. The tank is full of thousands of other, smaller, slower fish, which do not panic as the sharks cruise by.

Each time a great shark slides by and pauses inches from my head, my eyes meet its small lemon-yellow eye fixed on me. His ever-open jaws display rows of teeth. My eyes are unable to circumscribe, survey, foresee what his eye sees. I feel my eyes and my soul and big bloated body utterly exposed to that pale unreflecting eye. It is by circumscribing, foreseeing, and manipulating that human apes have taken possession of every square meter of Earth's surface, subjugating and exterminating all the other species. Sharks, virtually unchanged through three Ice Ages, are lords of the deep by virtue of the incomparable perfection of their bodies. They are less tigers than vultures; not their eyes but their electrical sense detects the spasmodic movements of sick and dying fish, which they feed on, assimilating them into the perpetual movement of their lives. I have nothing to fear.[4]

Yet there is the absolute certainty that the shark and I are looking at one another, that our eyes communicate. The shark's eyes are immobile and inexpressive; our eyes in their liquid sockets are as restless as their bodies. We have had to work to make our eyes fearful and wary, to force them to circumscribe, survey, and foresee. In the gaze of the shark, my

eyes lose their industriousness and return to their primal and
infantile delight.

In Cairo I met Wael, a young refugee from Sudan. He took
me to where he stays. It was in the middle of a vast wasteland
that had been the city garbage dump for centuries, so polluted
that not a weed was to be seen anywhere. Here the most destitute of Cairo's poor make bricks and pots out of the muck.
The terrain was pitted to hold basins of water and adjacent
basins of wet clay, and the brickmakers and potters themselves
live in caves excavated in the muck or mud-wall huts covered
with scavenged sheets of rusted metal. Their mud brick kilns
are above and below these hovels, the black smoke that seeps
from them hovering low overhead. It was like ground zero
after the end of urban civilization. The substance of the muck
is everywhere up against them, all their movements held in
it, their glances and their touch ending in it, their thoughts
inescapably terrestrial. I cast only oblique glances at them,
apprehensive less of the aggressions against foreigners that had
been so much in the press than of the resentment of the down-
trodden everywhere when their homes and their destitution
are stared at by well-to-do outsiders. But we went inside one
of these hovels. Wael's mother, to welcome me, poured from a
jug some water in a cup of clay. I suddenly thought I had been
transported to ground zero where civilization began—for the
first things humans made with their hands were pots fashioned
of clay. Cupped hands lifting water to the mouth were the first
pots, and the first pots of clay were made to hold that gesture.

Beyond this wasteland, I could see the dunes of Giza and
the pyramids. The next day I went there. Everyone has seen
them so often, in pictures in books, in films, in news broad-
casts, in cigarette ads; the images and impressions collected
on the surfaces of my eyes, ears, and skin while wandering
among them had already all been projected there many times
already. Beyond these images and impressions, I tried to sense

what the pyramids are. In grade school and in the books I now read they were identified as tombs of kings who had divinized themselves—the colossal monuments of a monstrous excrescence of egoism. Which is to view them as did the barbarian grave robbers (not the last of these barbarian chieftains was Howard Carter, who sold half the plunder from Pharaoh Tutankhamen to the New York Metropolitan Museum for fourteen thousand pounds sterling). One could just as well describe a medieval cathedral as a mausoleum for a lord bishop or king on the argument that their tombs are found in them. These mammoth constructions are some kind of cosmic markers. Their essential function is to do something in the cosmos. But virtually all the coordinates of the cosmos in which they are set are incomprehensible.

When the midday heat drove the tourists to their buses and the air-conditioned restaurants, I headed for the entrance of the great pyramid of Khufu. The Egyptian guides had already retreated to the shade of palm trees, but some of them saw me and rushed toward me. I paid them for a guided tour if they let me enter alone; each only wanted a few dollars. I was able to spend two hours alone inside. The tomb room is astonishingly small, bare, and unsculptured and not at the real center of the pyramid. The now-empty sarcophagus is a plain stone box. I did not detect any hint of the pharaoh's ghost in that chamber; what confronted me was the enormous reality of the stone above and about and below.

Napoleon calculated that there was enough stone in the three great pyramids of Giza to build a wall ten feet high and a foot wide around France. The stones were not cut at the quarries in uniform blocks; they are of varying sizes and their sides of varying angles. They were cut to fit one another at the site and were there fitted together so exactly that one cannot slip a knife between them. They were fitted together that painstakingly not only on the outer face of the pyramid, but in all the tiers, all the way through. Something utterly transcendent,

something of incalculable value, was sensed in stone, something to which all the energies and years of life of a laborer
could be devoted.

I went up the Nile to Luxor and the Valley of the Kings,
where later pharaohs were buried deep underground. I came
upon the tomb of Meneptah IV, little visited because floods
had pretty much destroyed the paintings, and once I entered
I found myself alone. The tunnel is very long and steep, several
hundred meters down. There is one landing halfway down,
and then at the bottom a very large pillared room cut in the
granite bedrock. In the center is the black sarcophagus in mint
condition. On the stone cover the face and folded hands of the
pharaoh are emerging from, or sinking into, the black stone.
I am invaded by a sense of a human life coming to rest deep
under millions of tons of rock. Here the surface agitations are
so remote from him, and, the few hours I linger there with him,
from me. I feel an imperative summons from the rock core of
the planet to stay, and feel the serene immobility and majestic
submission of the pharaoh to be an assignation.

V

Reticence

*D*ENKEN IST DANKEN, Martin Heidegger wrote: thought
is gratitude. Thanking consists in receiving with embracing hands what is given, holding it together, and showing it to,
sharing it with, others. Speaking and writing about what one
has seen, and experienced—what one has been given—can be
thoughtful, can be thankful. Thoughtful speaking and writing put forth the overall design and inner force of the data—
the given—detailing their aspects and inner relationships for
view, sharing them with others.

Thoughtfulness begins in opening one's heart to what is
given. It involves vulnerability and risk. Truth means seeing
what exceeds the possibility of seeing, what is intolerable to
see, what exceeds the possibility of thinking, Georges Bataille
wrote. "And I would not know *what is, what happens,* if I did
not know extreme pleasure, if I did not know extreme pain!"[1]

In speaking one can put oneself forth, to counteract one's
sense of vulnerability. But in thoughtful speech one instead
seeks only to offer to others what one has been given to see. In
thoughtful writing one loses sight of oneself, and one writes
not for a distinct person but for anyone. For a reader I am only
a self-effaced one who offers what has been given to see and to
celebrate or suffer.

But gratitude—thoughtfulness—can also silence all talk.

It happens that in the night and the long loneliness of the

mountains, the desert, or the ice, the torments of your flesh move you to respond to a chance encounter with another oblivion-seeker. You have no language in common, can say nothing to one another. Someone without civic and urban identity, someone denuded of her or his personal history, offers her or his body, abyss of unmarked wounds and dark exhilarations. You abandon yourself to monstrous kisses and caresses. You denude yourself and give yourself over to the strange passions of a stranger; you give yourself over to the risks of strangling, rape, ill-treatment, insults, cries of hatred, or unleashing of whole, deadly passions. You lose yourself in bestial and reptilian passions. You part without compensation or exaction. You do not talk about it when you are again among those of your own language.

How is it that the most intense voluptuous pleasures we are given induce in us reticence and silence? When it is not a stranger but someone you can communicate with very well, indeed someone you live with, who gives you most totally his or her voluptuous body, talk then too is silenced.

Of course words are common words, fashioned not for particular realities but for the general and recurrent lines of things and events. Yet it is not in words that we speak but in phrases and sentences, and one would be hard pressed to find, in a year of newspapers or a year of recorded conversation, any thoughtful sentence repeated. Of course we designate things so roughly, while Faulkner delineates out of the vast resources of his vocabulary the precise contours of an event or feeling. But so often the briefest expression—"O wow!"—expresses what is wondrous before us while the most loquacious description turns into an exhibition of the wit and verbal virtuosity of the speaker.

Writers take language seriously; indeed language is serious, though its seriousness can be broken by laughter. Writers call what they do work. Perhaps they only mean to suggest that they earn their wages as much as engineers or construction laborers.

Yet language has an inner kinship to work. Work is the progressive and sequential expenditure of energy for the sake of a
goal, a product, a future. Language formulates our experience
in successive units, in words and phrases, which shape time
into sequential moments. The speech or writing that aims to
make sense of some experience puts it into a context, evaluates
it, formulates what good it is or how it might be put to use.
The words do not end with a formulation and say of it that it
is of no use, that nothing follows from it. The sentence calls
for a sequel, another sentence that qualifies it, that justifies
it or supplies evidence for it, that builds on it, that draws out
a consequence, a conclusion, that evokes an objection to it.
The next sentence it invokes and requires will make use of it.
In addition, every utterance also depends for its meaning on
the prior utterances, and holds on to them. Nothing is lost.
Language, like work, is acquisition, appropriation, possession.

But is not experience itself appropriation? To experience
something is not simply for a succession of sensory patterns to
drift by. Our look goes out toward something appearing in the
environment and sets it in a relationship with ourselves. We
will use it to find other things, or we will hold on to it, keep it
in mind for future use.

But there are experiences in which the intentions and
designs on things we have formed are effaced. We embrace
and give ourselves over to what is given. We go out West just
to contemplate the inhuman grandeur of the Grand Canyon.
We go to sail the oceans, to dive the coral seas. We run off
cliffs to paraglide the winds. We go to California just to see
the giant sequoias. They make us stand tall and we open our
hearts to them.

The grandeur of the giant sequoias diminishes our sense
of ourselves; especially it renders derisory and shameful any
initiatives we could conceive to subordinate the trees to our
uses. The future that we project before us to furnish with our
goals and to give purpose and meaning to the things within

reach, *our* future, fades away before the formidable presence of the sequoias. The past too, which contains the decisions and resolutions that organize our dedication to the tasks at hand, disconnects. Even the preparations and plans for our trip to California to see the sequoias, all the arrangements that have to be made, the weariness of hundreds of miles of driving—all that sinks into insignificance and is gone. We find ourselves adrift in the present, soaring. However wearying is our trek in the mountains where they silently ascend to the skies, it is the opposite of labor. And all the notions and information we have accumulated about them dissipate before the skybound materiality of their presence. Such moments are ephemeral. When we leave their presence, we cannot reinstate it in a representation. Our visit has taken nothing from them.

In the embrace of a stranger one is no longer a professor, a virile and self-determined agent, one is infantile, being babied, one is a lusty and anonymous animal. In voluptuous transport one forgets oneself, loses sight of one's reputation, one's good name, one's dignity, one's identity, one's very body that is no longer one's own, moved by another, given to another. One learns nothing in voluptuous ravishments, takes nothing from them, one wastes time. The present swoons in on itself, intensifies and consumes itself. These experiences do not build on one another; the craving to lose oneself in orgasmic exultation is a repetition compulsion.

Rousing up things to do, to fix, to accomplish, to achieve dissipates these experiences. But these experiences also disconnect those agitations, those initiatives. Starting up a verbalization—asking oneself what is going on, what good it is and how good, what it means—already dissipates the ecstasy of the present. The most intense joys we are given empty the mind, extinguish the ego, and silence the greedy work of words. If decades later I happen to meet again the now-old woman or old man whom I met by chance and made love with long ago, we shall remember together those passionate transports as among the most wonderful gifts life gave us. Seated together on the veranda as night comes again, the remembering will silence us.

Twenty-four hours a day television news channels double up floods, volcanic explosions, earthquakes, battles in far-off countries, deaths of celebrities, and winnings at lotteries with photographic and verbal reports. Psychotherapists with their notebooks and tape recorders; sociologists with their questionnaires; historians sifting through acts of legislative bodies, court records, property assessments for tax purposes, and sales reports; and chroniclers of sports events and local news in newspapers prolong all significant events in individual and collective histories with reports and commentary. This frenetic production of language inevitably makes everything available for use: civil unrest in remote lands will be noted by corporate investors, the obituary columns will be read by funeral directors and estate lawyers, archaeological discoveries of incomplete skeletons of unknown humans dead ten thousand years ago will attract the attention of the tourism industry.

Yet the extreme experiences, the events for which we are most grateful, are harbored by silence.

This silence is not empty; in it lacks and wants are overfilled by gratitude. Gratitude is generous. We shall want to lead others to these oases of welcome, others we shall never know and from whom we can expect nothing in return. We shall have to tell them how to prepare and plan for their trip to California to see the sequoias, help them with all the arrangements that have to be made, and laugh over, so that they laugh over, the weariness of hundreds of miles of driving. Truth means seeing what exceeds the possibility of seeing, what is intolerable to see, what exceeds the possibility of thinking.

Notes

FACADES

1. Clifford Geertz, *Negara: The Theatre State in Nineteenth-Century Bali* (Princeton: Princeton University Press, 1980).

2. Johann Ludwig Burckhardt, *Travels in Syria and the Holy Land* (London: John Murray, 1822), 428–29.

3. Edward Robinson, *Biblical Researches in Palestine, Mount Sinai, and Arabia Petraea* (Boston: Crocker and Brewster, 1856).

RINGS

1. Claude Lévi-Strauss, "Introduction à l'oeuvre de Marcel Mauss," in Marcel Mauss, *Sociologie et anthropologie* (Paris: Presses Universitaires de France, 1960), xlvii–xlviii.

A MAN

1. "She was no longer a girl—she showed herself a woman." "She is a real woman." What qualities, deeper than cultural, broader than biological, are being recognized? There are those unfeminine women in Faulkner, shying away from none of the work their men do, who, at decisive moments, show themselves to be women. There are crisp, coolheaded, successful business executives who, at some moment of crisis in their own lives or in the lives of people dependent on them, proved to be women. There are nurses in wartime and in refugee camps, there are nuns, who at some decisive and revealing moments, show themselves to be women. To become a woman is not simply to be biologically female and maturing, and

it is not a program, construction, or performance, like making oneself feminine.

Does not the project of deconstructing the social construction of virility involve the judgment that virility—just like womanhood and the figures of outlaw, desperado, punk, street-smart adolescent, drag queen, queer—is an evaluative category constructed for its perceived social benefits? But before any ethical or social judgment, we must first understand the passionate force that cares about being virile and having a real man for a buddy—and that cares about being a real woman, a queer, a drag queen . . .

We further have to understand how passion communicates. It is not the category, implanted in the language and practices of a culture, that propagates virility. It is virility that communicates virility to others; it is heroism that ignites heroism; it is carnivalesque high-spiritedness that spreads carnivalesque high-spiritedness.

2. John Hersey, *A Single Pebble* (New York: Knopf, 1963), 100–101.

3. Manuel Puig, *The Kiss of the Spider Woman,* trans. Thomas Colchie (New York: Vintage, 1991), 63.

UNDERSTANDING

1. Procopius, *De aedificiis;* cited in Heinz Kähler and Cyril Mango, *Hagia Sophia* (New York: Praeger, 1967), 35.

THE DREADFUL MYSTIC BANQUET

1. Maurice Merleau-Ponty, *Phenomenology of Perception,* trans. Colin Smith (London: Routledge and Kegan Paul, 1962), 341.

2. Slavoj Žižek, *Looking Awry: An Introduction to Jacques Lacan through Popular Culture* (Cambridge, Mass.: MIT Press, 1992), 156–57.

3. Although the essential of the vision is in the silent, silencing epiphany, most of what we know as visions comes to us from texts—from sacred writings, epic poets, mystic writings, the literature of Joyce and Beckett, the speeches of Che Guevara and Nelson Mandela. There is a language, then, that conveys vision—epic, prophetic, visionary language. There is also a presence of language in the vision itself—language reduced to utterance, to invocation and appeal. Here the voice calls upon a nonhuman interlocutor. The incantatory force of his voice is cast in ritual formulas and repetitions; his own

individual voice is enveloped and lost in anonymous chants. Very often his voice calls up visible beings who have voices and who may be only voices.

4. Alexandra David-Neel, *Magic and Mystery in Tibet* (New York: Dover, 1971), 148–52.

5. Ibid., 150–51.

6. The red meal and the black meal of *chöd* is a vision from remote old Tibet, as far removed from our lives, our interactions, our institutions, and our traditions as possible. The vision emerges in the midst of a ritual for which there is long and disciplined preparation prescribed in Tibetan books and initiatory traditions. But a vision is what breaks through practical ways of living, institutions, and traditions. For a vision to take hold, it must not only break through the crust of our axioms, maxims, formulas, conceptual paradigms, and representations and impose itself in the radiance of its epiphany; it must also pull at the anchors of our practice. What is it about Ireland and Irish Catholicism that made the visions of Milton and Dante take hold of James Joyce? What is it about life in our high-tech archipelago that makes Joyce captivate us but not Milton or Dante?

THE RETURN OF EXTINCT RELIGIONS

1. Claude Lévi-Strauss, *Tristes Tropiques* (Paris: Plon, 1955), 478.

2. Ibid.

3. Friedrich Nietzsche, "Second Essay," in *On the Genealogy of Morals,* trans. Walter Kaufmann (New York: Vintage, 1969), §1.

4. Friedrich Nietzsche, *The Gay Science,* trans. Walter Kaufmann (New York: Vintage, 1974), §345.

5. "The most comprehensive soul, which can run and stray and roam farthest within itself; the most necessary soul, which out of sheer joy plunges itself into chance; the soul which, having being, dives into becoming; the soul which *has,* but *wants* to want and will; the soul which flees itself and catches up with itself in the widest circle; the wisest soul, which folly exhorts most sweetly; the soul which loves itself most, in which all things have their sweep and countersweep and ebb and flood—oh, how should the highest soul not have the worst parasites?" Friedrich Nietzsche, *Thus Spoke Zarathustra,* trans. Walter Kaufmann (New York: Penguin, 1980), 208–9.

6. "Opinions, along with all proofs, refutations, and the whole intellectual masquerade, are merely symptoms of the change in taste and most certainly not what they are still often supposed to be, its causes.

"What changes the general taste? The fact that some individuals who are powerful and influential announce without any shame, *hoc est ridiculum, hoc est absurdum,* in short, the judgment of their taste and nausea. . . . The reason why these individuals have different feelings and tastes is usually to be found in some oddity of their life style, nutrition, or digestion, perhaps a deficit or excess of inorganic salts in their blood and brain; in brief, in their *physis*. They have the courage to side with their *physis* and to heed its demands down to the subtlest nuances. Their aesthetic and moral judgments are among these 'subtlest nuances' of the *physis*." Nietzsche, *The Gay Science,* §39.

7. Ibid., §55.

8. Ibid., §10.

9. "The illumination and the color of all things have changed. We no longer understand altogether how the ancients experienced what was most familiar and frequent—for example, the day and waking. Since the ancients believed in dreams, waking appeared in a different light. The same goes for the whole of life, which was illumined by death and its significance; for us "death" means something quite different. All experiences shone differently because a god shone through them. All decisions and perspectives on the remote future, too; for they had oracles and secret portents and believed in prophecy. 'Truth' was experienced differently, for the insane could be accepted formerly as its mouthpiece—which makes *us* shudder or laugh.

"Every wrong had a different effect on men's feelings; for one feared divine retribution and not merely a civil punishment and dishonor. What was joy in ages when one believed in devils and tempters? What was passion when one saw demons lying in wait nearby? . . .

"We have given things a new color; we go on painting them continually. But what do all our efforts to date avail when we hold them against the colored splendor of that old master—ancient humanity?" Ibid., §152.

10. Ibid., §357.

11. Daniel Paul Schreber, *Memoirs of My Nervous Illness,* trans. Ida Macalpine and Richard A. Hunter (New York: New York Review Books, 2000).

12. "Art raises its head where the religions relax their hold. It takes over a host of moods and feelings engendered by religion, lays them to its heart and itself grows more profound and soulful, so that it is now capable of communicating exultation and enthusiasm as it formerly could not. The wealth of religious feelings, swollen to a torrent, breaks forth again and again and seeks to conquer new regions: but the growth of the Enlightenment undermined the dogmas of religion and inspired a fundamental distrust of them: so that the feelings expelled from the sphere of religion by the Enlightenment throw themselves into art; in individual cases into political life as well, indeed even straight into the sciences. Wherever we perceive human endeavours to be tinted with a higher, gloomier colouring, we can assume that dread of spirits, the odour of incense and the shadows of churches are still adhering to them." Friedrich Nietzsche, *Human, All Too Human,* trans. R. J. Hollingdale (Cambridge: Cambridge University Press, 1986), vol. 1, §150.

13. "Oh if the poets would only be again what they were once supposed to have been:—*seers* who tell us something of the *possible*! . . . If only they would let us feel in advance something of the *virtues of the future*! Or of virtues that will never exist on earth, though they could exist somewhere in the universe—of purple-glowing galaxies and whole Milky Ways of beauty! Astronomers of the ideal, where are you?" Friedrich Nietzsche, *Daybreak,* trans. R. J. Hollingdale (Cambridge: Cambridge University Press, 1997), §551.

14. Friedrich Nietzsche, *The Will to Power,* trans. Walter Kaufmann and R. J. Hollingdale (New York: Random House, 1967), §1038.

15. "It required the poets, existing outside the religious cult and the spell of religious *awe,* to accustom the imagination of men to acceding to such a thing: overweighed again by more pious moods and moments, however, this liberating influence of the poets again withdrew and the sacred remained, as before, in the realm of the monstrous, uncanny and quite specifically non-human. . . . The

oldest image of the god is supposed to *harbour and at the same time conceal* the god—to intimate his presence but not expose it to view. No Greek ever truly *beheld* his Apollo as a wooden obelisk, his Eros as a lump of stone; they were symbols whose purpose was precisely to excite fear of beholding him. The same applies to those wooden idols furnished with paltry carvings of individual limbs, sometimes an excess of them: such as a Spartan Apollo with four hands and four ears. In the incompleteness, allusiveness or overladenness of these figures there lies a dreadful holiness which is supposed to *fend off* any association of them with anything human. . . . —Only when, in the secular world of competition outside the religious cult, joy in the victory in the contest had risen so high that the waves here produced flooded over into the lake of the religious sensations; only when the statue of the victor was set up in the courts of the temples and the eye and the soul of the pious frequenter of the temple had, willingly or unwillingly, to accustom itself to this inescapable sight of *human* strength and beauty, so that, standing thus close to one another, spatially and in the soul, reverence for man and reverence for god came to blend together: only then was the fear of an actual humanization of the divine image also overcome and the great arena for plastic art in the grand style opened up: yet still with the restriction that wherever *worship* was to be conducted the ancient forms and ugliness were preserved and scrupulously imitated." Nietzsche, *Human, All Too Human,* vol. 2, §222.

16. Ibid., vol. 1, §129.

LALIBELA

1. Ewald Hein and Brigitte Kleidt, *Ethiopia—Christian Africa,* trans. John M. Deasy (Ratingen: Melina-verlag, 1999), 110–11.

VODOU

1. FRAPH (Front for the Advancement and Progress of Haiti) is a paramilitary organization founded by Emmanuel "Toto" Constant in 1993. Since 1991 Constant had been a paid asset at the CIA. In December 1994 he fled to the United States.

2. Georges Bataille, *Oeuvres complètes* (Paris: Gallimard, 1973), 6:296–97.

BREAKOUT

1. Georges Bataille, *Visions of Excess,* trans. Allan Stoekl (Minneapolis: University of Minnesota Press, 1985), 13.

2. Ibid.

3. The Grand Canyon of the Colorado is 1,638 meters at its deepest; here the Colca Canyon is 4,174 meters deep.

4. Humans are not a natural food for sharks. Ancient maps of the ocean depict the sea monsters that so terrified Columbus's sailors, but there are no sharks among them. Sharks came to feed on humans twice in recorded history: the first was during the slave trade. The ships, loaded with Africans, took months to cross the Atlantic; very often tropical storms hit them. They rode out the storms by putting everybody in the hold and sealing the hatch. Captains' logs tell of opening the hatch days later and throwing the suffocated dead into the sea: "What a feast for the sharks!" The second time was during the First World War, when submarines torpedoed ships and cast hundreds of bleeding bodies into the sea.

RETICENCE

1. Bataille, *Oeuvres complètes,* 3:12, 10.

ALPHONSO LINGIS is professor emeritus of philosophy at Pennsylvania State University. He is the author of *The Community of Those Who Have Nothing in Common, Dangerous Emotions, Foreign Bodies, Abuses, Excesses: Eros and Culture,* and *Deathbound Subjectivity.* His work has been translated into French, Italian, Japanese, Turkish, and Lithuanian.